DEAF CHILDREN,
THEIR FAMILIES AND PROFESSIONALS

Deaf Children, Their Families and Professionals

Dismantling Barriers

Sarah Beazley and Michele Moore

David Fulton Publishers
London

David Fulton Publishers Ltd
2 Barbon Close, London WC1N 3JX

First published in Great Britain by
David Fulton Publishers 1995

Note: The right of Sarah Beazley and Michele Moore to be identified as the author of this work has been asserted by them in accordance with the Copyright, Designs and Patents Act 1988.

British Library Cataloguing in Publication Data

A catalogue record for this book is available from the British Library

ISBN 1-85346-354-X

Typeset by Textype Typesetters, Cambridge
Printed in Great Britain by BPC Wheatons Ltd, Exeter

Contents

Acknowledgements

We would like to thank all the families who made this book possible. These include the deaf children and their parents, brothers and sisters who welcomed us into their homes and so willingly shared their experiences; the families who wrote to us to give us their stories with openness and trust; and our own long-suffering families for their encouragement, understanding and support.

We also wish to extend our thanks to the production team of *TALK*, the official publication of the National Deaf Children's Society, for providing a means of contacting deaf children and their families across the country.

The people who helped us with transcriptions, and with technical back-up, are too numerous to list but they will know who they are, and that we are ever grateful for the hours of work involved.

Foreword

In recent years, disabled people have argued that the major problems they face are the result of external barriers of all kinds, whether they be economic, social, environmental, educational or communicative. This analysis has come to be known as the social model of disability and has provided a fertile framework for the analysis of most areas of disabled people's lives.

However, the social model has not been used in any systematic or coherent way to discuss family life where one or other member may have an impairment, that is, until this book was written. The authors are to be congratulated for taking this important step in their study of the lives of families with a deaf child.

Because of this application of the social model, the book is important not just to families with deaf children and the professionals who work with them but to anyone who has an interest in disability issues.

The authors attempt to write in a non-disabling way for anyone who might read it: it is accessible to parents while still saying things that are relevant and constructive for professional practice, even if this might make those professionals who read it somewhat uncomfortable.

The study makes an important contribution to newly emerging participative research methodologies in that it places the parents' view of the world at the centre of the analysis and in so doing, articulates the kinds of changes they think are necessary to improve the quality of life for their families and themselves.

The book has made a lasting contribution to a previously misunderstood and neglected area and deserves to be widely read.

Mike Oliver
Professor of Disability Studies
University of Greenwich

CHAPTER 1
Deaf Children, Their Families and Professionals

What this book is about

This book is about the importance of placing the views of families with deaf children at the front of policies and practices which impact on their lives. It concerns such families in a variety of different situations and circumstances, facing a whole range of issues, many of which are equally relevant to children with other impairments and their families. The aim of the book is to raise awareness of how enabling environments can be provided for deaf children and their families. It is about taking disability out of their experience of hearing impairment.

Background

The 1994 conference proceedings, 'Keeping Deaf Children in Mind', present some of the dilemmas raised when we think about the situation of deaf children and their families (Laurenzi and Hindley, 1994). One debate the editors consider is 'Are deaf children disabled, should we think about their development in terms of what they can't do? Or arc deaf children provisional members of the Deaf community and so different rather than disabled?' (1994). These are important questions for anyone connected with deaf children and their families and we felt we should spell out our perspective right at the beginning of this book.

We feel that deaf children are, by virtue of hearing impairment, 'different' from children who are not deaf. One way in which deaf children are different from their hearing peers is certainly in their right to prospective membership of the Deaf Community, and we agree with Laurenzi and Hindley that it is essential to recognise this important dimension of a deaf child's identity from the outset. We have a different way of looking at the question of whether deaf children are *disabled*, however. In this book we will argue that deaf children very often are disabled. But in a slightly different vein from Laurenzi and Hindley, we think disability has absolutely nothing to do with what deaf children themselves can't do. We wholeheartedly reject any outlook which views deaf children's development *'in terms of what they can't do'* (1994). We argue that deaf children can *be disabled*; we do not however, think that deaf children *have disabilities*. In our view, deaf children have hearing impairment, and other people *enable* or *disable* them and their families, depending on how they behave and what values underpin their attitudes.

Ideas about the way in which the experience of disability is socially produced have been developed by disabled writers themselves, notably Oliver (1990, 1993a), Finkelstein (1993) and French (1993). This theme is most usefully applied to an understanding of the situations of deaf children and their families and enables us to see that barriers to inclusion are not within the child. Hearing impairment is not the central problem which faces deaf children and their families. We view disabling barriers and oppressive environments which undermine deaf children's chances of an ordinary and fulfilled life as the major problem. Thus we talk about deaf children as disabled by other people who make life difficult for them and their families; disabled by assessment procedures which fail to pick up that they are deaf; disabled by a school's failure to provide a satisfactory communication environment; disabled by professionals who insist they know better than the child's own parents what would help them; disabled by segregation and so on. These are all ways in which a child with hearing impairment can be disabled by other people's attitudes and oppressive environments. Therefore we are arguing deaf children do not have disabilities, rather disability is something imposed upon them and their families by inadequate support. Stories families told us also provide many opportunities for showing how, when other people are enabling, deaf children and their families are not disabled and have access to exactly the same activities, achievements and aspirations as anyone else.

Our argument is that deaf children are disabled if other people have prejudicial attitudes towards them and towards their potential achievements. We argue that deaf children can be disabled by oppressive social and educational practices, by professionals who disempower both them and their families, and by any individual or group who, or which, is intolerant of difference and refuses to celebrate diversity. In short then, we argue throughout this book that deaf children and their families can indeed be disabled, and profoundly disabled too, but this has nothing to do with the fact of a child's hearing impairment. Intolerant people and oppressive environments *disable* deaf children and here, we think about deaf children and disability in terms of what everyone else, beyond the child, can or can't, and does or doesn't, do. We agree with Laurenzi and Hindley (1994) that it is completely unhelpful to think about deaf children in terms of what they themselves can't do.

The book makes a plea for readers to recognise their own role in the production of disablement for deaf children and their families. Families who spoke to us are challenging readers to think about how they can change what they do, so to produce enabling environments and support which is not oppressive. This sometimes makes the book an uncomfortable read. In parts, it proves disconcerting because we have recounted the stories families told in order to provide them with a vehicle for self-expression rather than to protect the sensitivities of those whom the stories are sometimes about. We feel that not to have done so, while much safer for us as writers, would have been a betrayal. If a particular passage does jar, it might be worth stopping to think why, and also to reflect upon the roots of one's agitation.

Throughout the book families with deaf children describe how they encounter potentially devastating crises, often harrowing encounters with other people and endless episodes of struggle in isolation as they battle for opportunities which would give them an ordinary life. What we argue is that these ordeals have surprisingly little to do with a child's hearing impairment yet everything to do with the way in which other people, especially (but not only) professionals, respond to deaf children and their families. We are certain of this because when a family's story is characterised by positive responses and enabling circumstances then the fact that a child has a hearing impairment is not necessarily associated with any crises other than those which ordinarily appear in any family with children from time to time.

How we assembled this book

The content of each chapter emerges from many hours of talking with families, and the material we present consists in direct reporting of their reflections. We rely heavily upon the words of the families who took part to add new perspectives to what has previously been written about their situations and experiences. Quotations are mainly taken from face-to-face interviews, and we add passages from letters, diaries and poems too, where these reveal more about the realities of family life when a child is deaf. A brief outline of the context in which the research came about, together with a description of our approach is presented next.

The families who took part

The families whose stories are represented in this book all experience family life with a deaf child. In other respects, the families are quite different from each other. The accounts which provide the main basis for this book, are those of a small handful of families who were the first to reply to a notice published in the magazine of the National Deaf Children's Society, inviting people to take part in the research (*TALK*, 1992). Those who came forward were all hearing parents of deaf children. One family was part of a cultural and linguistic minority group. The pattern of responses immediately raises important questions about the type of families whose views we are presenting and this is an important issue. Obviously we do not claim our small sample is in any way representative of families with deaf children generally, but we would add that there is no reason to suppose the material gives an atypical snap-shot. The families differed greatly, not only in geographical, social and material circumstances, but also in their reasons for choosing to take part in interviews. Their stories are amplified and extended by reflections of others who contributed to the project through writing.

Many times, one family's problems would be retold by another whose circumstances were totally different, except that they too had a deaf child in the family. Many readers will have heard or been involved in similar stories themselves, perhaps on numerous occasions. The continual echoes between anecdotes affirm the authenticity of those we recount in this book. When we started talking to families with deaf children, the complexity of what happens to them and the directness with which they could recall often painful chains of events, was immediately striking. The same preoccupations were repeated to us time and time again by different families and these vividly reveal the ease with which, without perhaps anyone having any awareness of doing so, a child's hearing impairment can be turned into a lifelong experience of disability – disabling not just for the deaf child, but often for the whole family too.

Critics will say the accounts are retrospective and memories are only partial; they are invariably selective and may be distorted, even inaccurate. Even so, we have been told the things that have stuck most in a family's mind. If professionals would recount the same events differently, then the mismatch between their version of events and the version which has stayed with a family is, no doubt, very revealing. In addition, some episodes which families discussed were not retrospective, but concern ongoing events and situations, and sometimes prospective events.

Another criticism could be that perhaps the families who volunteered to take part were the sort who like to protest loudly and that many other families who are content with the support they receive, simply did not come forward. This is plainly not the case. Families who took part did so for very different reasons, not least for some, because they felt they were getting good support and it would benefit others to know about it. We felt it would be helpful to specify the motivations for taking part to help forestall this reproach.

Reasons for taking part

Most families wanting to take part felt that by doing so they might help others:

> **Jenny:** everything is quite normal that we are doing and we are experiencing ... I think [families] just need reassuring [and] we've come a long way. ... I would be more than willing to help you.... Chloe was eventually diagnosed as profoundly deaf at 22 months. She is now ten years old and we have reached all sorts of obstacles and hurdles on the way. Our main regret is that when we truly needed help and support or other parents to talk to we hadn't anything. Your world is shattered when you learn one of your children is disabled. I have lots to tell and hopefully all information you amass for your studies will benefit others.

As well as participating in an interview, Jenny contributed her personal diary to the project, again with a view to helping others:

> **Jenny:** you see as I wrote these things, I was experiencing these things at the time .. just they might be little things that .. whatever, if it's of any help to anybody.

Other motivations were similar:

> **Paula:** I feel by helping you, [we] might benefit others in some way, however small. That would be a bonus for us.

Two families wanted to address specific issues of ongoing concern:

> **Eleanor:** Rachel is a bright happy child who keeps up with her peers and enjoys school. We have encountered many problems and frustrations along the way, both at school and at home and would be happy to share them with you. Our two concerns at the moment are (i) that as a 'mainstreamer' she has very little contact with other deaf children, (ii) her transfer to secondary education.

> **Graham:** we too have a story to tell, it involves a deaf child, the DHSS, ourselves and of course, money. Our story started 870 days ago and will continue for a lot longer, during that time we have had a few skirmishes but the biggest battle is yet to come.

Most participants simply felt it would be productive to share experiences:

> **Foster mother** (anon): I have learned a lot, in case it is any use for your project.

> **Gillian:** I would like to tell you about an incident when my daughter was four and first went to school, one of the first pictures she brought home was of her family, Mum and Dad, two younger brothers and herself, all drawn as normal

... except Siân [see front cover]. This is the only time she has mentioned her ears, mostly she is very matter of fact about them. At the time she had only had her hearing aids nine months and drawing was one of her main enjoyments. ... If you are covering all of the UK in your research we would be interested in taking part.

Helen: I would like to take part in your project involving Deaf children and their families. Our daughter Katy is 23 years old with a wealth of experiences to discuss.

Characteristics of families interviewed

Pseudonyms are given for all members of the families interviewed who were living at home at the time of the research, or to whom informants refer by name.

Informants: Helen (mother), Andrew (father) and Katy
Deaf child: Katy, aged 23, living away from parental home. Helen contracted rubella during pregnancy and Katy was diagnosed as deaf at eight months.
Other immediate family: Martin and Stephanie (older siblings), living with parents.

Informants: Maureen (mother) and Graham (step-father)
Deaf child: Ian, aged 14, Ian was born prematurely and diagnosed as deaf at eight months.
Other immediate family: Robert and Scott (younger brothers). Nine step-brothers and sisters living elsewhere.

Informants: Pat (mother) and Tony (father)
Deaf child: Christopher, aged ten. Christopher became deaf at the age of five, following meningitis. He had a cochlear implant at the age of nine, approximately twelve months prior to our meeting.
Other immediate family: one grown up half-brother living elsewhere.

Informants: Jenny (mother), Chloe, Joanna (older sister), Holly (younger sister) and Chantal (children's friend)
Deaf child: Chloe, aged ten. Following complications at birth, Chloe was diagnosed as deaf at 22 months.
Other immediate family: Doug (father) and Shelly (older sister).

Informants: Gillian (mother) and Siân
Deaf child: Siân, aged nine. Siân was diagnosed deaf at three years.
Other immediate family: Mike (father), Oliver and Dylan (younger brothers).

Informants: Eleanor (mother) and Rachel
Deaf child: Rachel, aged eight. Rachel was diagnosed deaf by the time she was 18 months.
Other immediate family: Brian (father), Richard and Simon (older brothers) and Hanna (younger sister).

Informant: Emma (mother)
Deaf child: Sam, aged two. Sam contracted meningitis in hospital soon after birth and was diagnosed deaf in the early months of his life.
Other family: Kevin (father), living elsewhere.

Three of the families lived in cities, two in remote rural areas, one in a large town and one in a small town. We mention this because subsequently, they experienced quite different types of service provision.

All of the thoughts participants shared with us are, of course, representative of their views at one particular time.

How we interviewed families

The way in which we collected the family stories is unusual. This is because we placed the families firmly in the driving seat when it came to deciding what they would talk about. This way of doing things is unusual in social research because researchers typically start off by assuming that some questions they are interested in will lead to the discovery of important and valuable facts. Most of the research in the field of support for families with deaf children has focused on issues which researchers have decided to prioritise in their investigations, and little scope has existed for parents to determine the issues of interest themselves (Gregory, 1976: 94; Nolan and Tucker, 1988). Our approach, however, has been to assume that families themselves would best know what kinds of issues researchers should be addressing, and so the agenda for the interviews was left open for the families to decide the topics of interest. Because we took this approach, the priority attached by families with deaf children to the issues we discuss is undeniable and we feel the material in the book therefore has a great deal to say to professionals and other families.

We started the interviews by saying that we were hoping to collect information which families with deaf children felt would be beneficial

8

for other such families, and service providers to know about. But other than that, we left the choice of topics to family members present. We confined our input as far as possible to prompting further exploration of things informants had already chosen to talk about, by using phrases such as 'can you tell us a bit more about that?' or 'how did that make you feel?'. Children present chipped in or wrote their ideas down for us. None of the families had any difficulty choosing their agenda. The shortest interview lasted around three hours, closing because children needed attending to, rather than because informants had run out of steam. Other interviews lasted up to six hours. Thus although the range of respondents may be small, the data is wide ranging, in-depth and above all, very rich.

There was a second strand to our research approach that is also important to mention. In addition to placing emphasis on uncovering issues which would be of maximum relevance to others, we wanted the research interviews also to be of benefit to those who took part. Our tactic for achieving this was to try and encourage links between what families were telling us and their own ideas for how change could be brought about, not just for themselves in their immediate situation, but also for other families in a wide variety of circumstances and positions. Thus the book includes many suggested strategies for bringing about change which were volunteered by families, and which result directly from their firsthand experiences. In both conducting the research interviews and writing this book we have tried to place emphasis on problem-solving through increased personal awareness and developing self-confidence.

We have attempted to link what families have to say, to real strategies for professionals and parents who might be prompted to re-examine aspects of their own ways of reacting to and dealing with the situation of deaf children and their families. Each chapter makes practical suggestions for parents and professionals who wish to re-think aspects of their own circumstances. We have aimed to present a detailed picture of experiences of families with deaf children in an accessible way, and to discuss these experiences in terms of important consequences both for those families and also for professionals who come into contact with them.

How the book is arranged

The book is divided into different phases of family life, rather than focusing on the whole life experience of one family at a time. We felt a chronological format would be the most helpful to other families as they can immerse themselves in parts of the book which connect with their own immediate situations. If it is daunting to think too far ahead parents can leave some of the chapters until later. Professionals on the other hand can find in this book the whole spectrum of family life with a deaf child.

In Chapter 2 we start by exploring the notion that other people's attitudes and unthinking behaviour can needlessly kick start personal tragedy when a family discovers their child is deaf. This sets the scene for the central drama often played out by professionals working with deaf children and their families, which is the focus of Chapter 3 and concerns how to get communication going. Here the question of 'who knows what's best?' takes centre stage in the lives of deaf children and their families, and the repercussions of decisions made about whether to sign or not to sign rebound in every subsequent chapter. We find these reverberations in Chapter 4, which addresses issues in school life and examines what deaf children and their families want from education. Decisions about how deaf children communicate have far-reaching implications for the parents' subsequent choice of school and Chapters 3 and 4 reveal that profound misgivings parents may experience in relation to these issues demand the highest level of integrity from professionals. Chapter 5 examines family life and ways in which deaf children and their families can be included or conversely, excluded, from the ordinary things that families with children generally like to do. In Chapter 6 we describe how images of, and assumptions about, deaf children and their families impact on the prospects for their hopes and dreams to come true. All of the chapters provide justification for the book's emphasis on the role professionals can play in minimising disablement.

We hope that by describing and analysing the detailed reflections of a small number of families, we can challenge some everyday assumptions and practices which shape what goes on in the lives of families with deaf children. Our final chapter reviews problems raised by the research project, and draws attention to ways in which deaf children, their families, researchers and professionals might together find new ways forward for more effective support.

Reasons for writing this book

Thus there are several reasons why we wrote this book. Firstly, we wanted to illustrate the variety of situations in which families with deaf children find themselves. We wanted to demonstrate the importance, through presenting what families with deaf children have to say for themselves, of placing their own reflections firmly at the front of policy and practice which claims to be about improving their situations. An important aim has been to try and provide practical ideas for children, their families and professionals who are interested in bringing about personal change and development – with the chapters suggesting practical steps for helping individuals to make headway with predicaments they may face. Finally we wanted to help progress an agenda for future development of family-friendly policy for deaf children and their families.

A note about language

As far as possible, the word 'deaf' has been spelt with a small 'd' when it describes the physical condition of deafness, and with a capital 'D' when it refers to the culture of Deaf people. We sometimes use the convention 'd/Deaf' as a way of making clear that both those who do, and those who do not, aspire to British Sign Language usage and associated cultural heritage are included in the reference. As the deaf children in this study all have hearing parents, deaf with a lower case 'd' is used when referring to children.

To aid the reader, we would also like to clarify that in quotations, two dots (..) indicate that the speaker pauses, and three dots (...) indicate that material has been left out.

CHAPTER 2

Discovering a Child is Deaf: Dismantling Personal Tragedy

Introduction

In this chapter we discuss the impact felt by families both at the time of discovery, and subsequently, as a result of the way they find out their child is deaf. We analyse the families' reflections on this subject using the idea put forward in Chapter 1. That is, that understanding the experience of a family with a deaf child involves looking at the complex relationship between the child's hearing impairment and the social situation in which they and their family find themselves.

Before presenting the stories of the families who were interviewed, it is necessary to introduce some of the common assumptions surrounding the discovery that a child is deaf, and also to explain why we suggest management of such a discovery has a critical influence on deaf children and their families thereafter.

Assumptions surrounding discovery

Psychological approaches to understanding the experience of families when they find out their child is deaf often suppose parents pass through a series of 'stages' of adjustment (Bench, 1992; Ogden, 1984). Some writers describe this as similar to the stages often associated with processes of bereavement (Webster, 1994). A process of grieving is anticipated in which the reactions of parents to the news their child is deaf are expected to be characterised by shock, denial, anger and depression. It is imagined 'parents of a deaf child grieve for the normal child they have lost and must be helped through a series of stages of coming to terms with such a loss' (Webster, 1994). There is a confusing expectation that parents need to respond to the news that their child is *deaf* in a similar way to if they had actually discovered that their child was *dead*. Ironically, parents who do not appear to go through the predicted signs of grieving risk incurring the scepticism of professionals who have been trained to expect bereavement-like reactions upon diagnosis of deafness. It can be seen how the expectation that parents will be devastated by the news of their child's hearing impairment can be used by professionals to justify the opinion that parents who take the news of their child's hearing impairment in any other way are failing to adjust, or denying their child is deaf. Attention has been drawn elsewhere to the danger that expectations of grief and despair can become prescriptive for deaf children and their families (Gregory, 1991).

Psychological theories of adjustment to impairment need to be resisted, not least because focus upon individual adaptation allows professionals to abdicate responsibility for the role they themselves can play in supporting families in positive ways through the realisation that their child has an impairment (Oliver et al., 1987). If professionals invest in the inevitability of processes of grieving, trauma and depression then they can excuse themselves if this is how parents react. The problem with the idea that there are inevitable stages in family adjustment, is that it sets up the *expectation* that parents will experience grief and feel utterly downhearted. Professionals using ideas about individual psychological stages to help them predict how families will react to the news that their child is deaf, can assume parents will be devastated and will see the future as characterised by grieving and facing up to loss. This means that if parents do turn out to feel abject misery, professionals do not have to worry themselves too much about whether this reaction has anything to do with service provision. In spite of these damaging implications, however, mainstream text books for those involved in support services for education, health, social services and the like, continue to take for granted that parents will respond in this way (Solity and Bickler, 1994).

Our concern is not to deny hearing impairment can have a profound impact upon a child and their family, but rather to point out that commonplace psychological approaches to managing disclosure of deafness can actually produce and reinforce a sense of personal tragedy. There can be no doubt that a child's hearing impairment is a significant determinant of the child's and family's identity and future, but whether the discovery of deafness need go hand-in-hand with grief and personal tragedy, for either the child or their family, is an entirely different matter.

It becomes impossible to see responses to the discovery of a child's hearing impairment as simply to do with personal adjustment, whether in individual or family terms. Our feeling is that a much wider set of adjustments is required which firstly, takes into account the personal situation of deaf children and their families, and secondly, makes explicit the necessity for identifying coping strategies that go beyond the capabilities of individuals or families. We have no doubt that professionals play a pivotal role in enabling a family to manage the discovery of their child's deafness, but feel reference to psychological models which place emphasis upon individual adjustment does a great disservice to deaf children and their families.

Before moving on to look at how the families in our study were told of their child's hearing impairment, it is worth taking a quick look at one or two of the possible reasons why professionals continue to fix upon ideas of individual and family adjustment.

Professionals and theories

Any view a professional chooses to put forward is supported by a climate of 'expertise' surrounding their work. The things professionals say to families are packaged in highly abstracted information and often bewildering academic theories. Professionals, after all, have usually spent years studying their subject in both university and clinical settings. Parents on the other hand, are likely to get to the point of finding out their child is deaf knowing, in comparison, relatively little about hearing impairment or audiology and other such specialist fields. Knowledge makes professionals powerful. The images of deaf children and their families which they present at the point of disclosing hearing impairment, are likely to be firmly and forever etched upon parents' minds.

Our concern is that when parents are just finding out their child is deaf, it is easy for them to be made very vulnerable. In turn, the more vulnerable parents are, then the more they will be dependent upon professionals. There is something of a 'catch 22' situation here. Some writers would even go so far as to suggest professionals have a vested interest in producing vulnerable families in order to assert their own importance and further their privileged careers (Dyson, 1987). Unfortunately, the things parents have told us about the way in which the diagnosis of their child's deafness was given, suggest this proposition might not be without foundation. We heard of many instances in which it is hard to interpret the way in which parents were told as doing anything other than instantly and permanently disabling deaf children and their families. It should be stressed that our interpretation of the evidence does not provide any kind of definitive proof that professionals behave in ways which produce dependence and vulnerability, rather we simply suggest the possibility that these may be outcomes of an uncritical approach to professionalism.

What we find in this chapter is that the context of disclosing a child's diagnosis of deafness provides considerable opportunities for promoting ·personal tragedy and for making families dependent upon professionals. Our contention is that this simply need not happen, and this idea will be used to examine the variety of ways in which parents taking part in our study found out their child was deaf. We aim to illuminate a variety of concerns that need to be addressed both by professionals who find themselves making disclosures of hearing impairment, and by parents who wish to reflect on their own experience.

At some point during the interviews the discussion invariably turned to the question of how families found out their child was deaf. The explanation was often a very long one, stretching on from first suspicions that 'something was wrong'. For some parents a specific occasion on which they were told could be described, but for others a series of disclosures led up to confirmation of their child's deafness. For at least one family, important issues to do with 'finding out' remained unresolved many years after the diagnosis of deafness was given.

When episodes and events surrounding disclosure of children's hearing impairment are examined in depth, it quickly becomes apparent that sometimes a family does appear to go through a series of stages. What we feel the interviews show, however, is these are not stages of individual psychological reactions based on personal grievance and loss. The stages of adjustment families have to go through are *socially constructed stages* in the sense that they are embedded in the circumstances in which a family find themselves, and also in other people's behaviour towards them. They are stages which are created out of the competencies or incompetencies of others, in particular, of professionals in relevant support agencies. If service providers are sensitive, well informed, well co-ordinated and efficient, then the stages of adjustment a family goes through upon learning their child is deaf are not invariably characterised by shock, denial, anger and depression. If, on the other hand, service providers come across as insensitive, disorderly, lacking knowledge and poorly co-ordinated, then it should come as no surprise to learn families experience feelings of devastation, grief and despair. The point is that these feelings do not arise because parents learn their child has a hearing impairment; they arise because barriers to coping are imposed by the very professionals who supposedly provide support and enable deaf children and their families.

Without doubt, the professional who discloses news of a child's hearing impairment is in a strong position to influence outcomes for the child and their family. Let's look at how this is so.

How the news is given

Pat and Tony's story of how they discovered their son is deaf clearly illustrates how professionals can create despondency and despair by the way in which they manage the process of letting parents know. Pat's description of the extent to which she had been able to anticipate hearing impairment provides a useful starting point for reflection.

Within a short time of Christopher regaining consciousness following a life-threatening episode of meningitis, Pat had made some unsettling observations:

> **Pat**: something wasn't right. I observed, and I thought 'something's not right .. he's different'.. He was such a good conversationalist. I thought 'I know he's been in a coma', but I thought 'well I know there's nothing wrong mentally because he's comprehending everything that's going on, he understands who everybody is'... I'd thought about all this and I thought 'there's nothing wrong with him, but he's not actually answering them for some reason'.

A nurse on the ward, herself a hearing aid user, recognised the parents' concerns:

> **Tony**: this nurse ... she banged something, didn't she .. and she actually gave me the pans, two big pans to stand behind him .. and I think really she was telling us nicely.

Shortly after this, unable to recall any other preparation from professionals and unaccompanied by Tony at the time, Pat recalls how the specialist imparted the diagnosis:

> **Pat**: Mr Roberts was the man who was going to tell me whether he was deaf or not. And I did nothing but wait about for this Mr Roberts and I thought 'well I don't want to miss him'. I'd spent nearly three weeks in hospital. I hadn't gone home and my mother and father-in-law came and said 'right go and get yourself a cup of tea and just have a little walk round and we'll stay with him for half and hour' .. and erm I went off and as I came back my father-in-law said, 'quick, quick, Mr Roberts is here. He's with Mum in such a room up there' so I ran up, I walked in. My mother-in-law said 'oh this is Mrs Kennedy, his mum' and he said 'hello' and I said 'hello Mr Roberts' so he said 'yes, your son's deaf'. Just like that. I mean it was absolutely ... it was the most horrendous conversation I've had with anybody in my life. The man was so busy he had so many people round him .. the man had got no idea of what I'd been told. He'd got no idea what I'd been waiting for. He had no conversation with me .. I just couldn't believe it .. I felt absolutely .. I can't describe how I felt. You know it was the most disgusting conversation I'd ever had and it felt like the end of the world.
>
> **Tony**: when Pat came home from hospital and said that she'd been to visit the specialist and he told her in the corridor and all this business, I felt very, very sympathetic because she was really upset. But I felt a lot of anger at the way it had been done. I wasn't angry because he was deaf, because we really knew he was already .. that's [anger] directed at the way she's been told.

For Pat the news *'felt like the end of the world'*. Not because Christopher had a hearing impairment, but because in finding out, she had been subjected to *'the most disgusting conversation'*. The professional with responsibility for imparting this colossal piece of information about her son had done so without setting aside a time or a place, without enabling the presence of both parents, without checking what they already knew, without offering adequate links with other service providers who might be able to help ... without even introducing himself to the child's mother. Clearly Pat could be expected to experience shock and despair. But not as a result of the so-called inevitable processes of adjustment to the news that her child is deaf; simply shock and despair created out of a lack of proper professional care. Pat and Tony's ideas on how things could have been handled better place very few demands on either the personal or practical resources of professionals:

> **Tony**: a little room .. all nicely decorated where you can go and sit down and talk about it.

Even within our small sample, Pat and Tony's experience was not unique. Jenny and her husband, Doug, were treated in an almost identical fashion when they found out their daughter is deaf:

> **Jenny**: the theatre sister ... she came out .. she told me .. she said that her middle ear was damaged and she would probably never hear. Just like that. Which I mean in one respect I appreciate that she was so honest with me but .. it was just complete shock
> **Interviewer**: and were you on your own?
> **Jenny**: with my husband, but he'd gone off then, he was looking after the other children.

These experiences illustrate why we are disillusioned with psychological theories which look for explanations of parents' reactions to their child's hearing impairment in terms of individual personal adjustments to significant life events. The importance of recognising social pressures and stressors in the parents' experience of finding out about their child's hearing impairment is crystal-clear if we think about the above two stories. The necessity for acknowledging that coping mechanisms involve not just individual members of the families, but professionals too, is paramount.

Counting dads in

All the families interviewed described a clear distinction in the way mothers and fathers are involved by professionals starting from the very initial stages of contact. Both families quoted above, indicate that involvement of fathers would appear to be considered an irrelevance when diagnosis of a child's hearing impairment is given. If fathers are rendered invisible by professionals they are quickly impoverished through lack of first-hand experience and accounts. The descriptions given by Pat and Jenny are worrying because where professionals expect only to relate with the mothers of hearing-impaired children, this can be profoundly disabling for the whole family (Wickham-Searle, 1992).

Pat and Jenny both stress that their partners were making every effort to figure prominently in their child's experience, but were excluded when the disclosure of hearing impairment was given. The exclusion of fathers at the point of first being told, immediately influences both the way in which, and the extent to which, they are subsequently involved, not only with professionals, but with their child too. What concerns us is that uncritical focus of attention on mothers may lead professionals to under-estimate the contribution fathers make to their child's development and damage their prospective involvement. If professionals curtail inclusion of fathers by, for example, not making sure they are present when diag-nosis is given, this has a prescriptive impact on the participation of the father in future. Service providers need to be alerted to the importance of including fathers as well as mothers in discussions of and decisions about their deaf children. Other writers have also appealed for professionals to stop leaving fathers out of dialogue which concerns their children and their lives (Hornby, 1992).

It seems important for professionals to guard against personal assump-tions about child care and how the family is organised. It may be worth considering whether child care and development is assumed to be solely the concern of women, and if so, whether this is an acceptable assump-tion to make. Different approaches to mothers and to fathers will give rise to different experiences for those parents and subsequently, to differ-ent patterns of involvement. There are several sources of potential disablement here. Mothers are disabled by being isolated and positioned at the sharp-end of everything to do with their hearing-impaired child, and fathers are disabled by being excluded and positioned as having only a peripheral role to play. This can have dramatic impact (Kluwin and Gaustad, 1991). In Pat and Tony's experience for example, Pat describes herself as having more emotional adjustment to face up to:

> **Pat**: I've probably been more angry than Tony has been about things. Tony has looked at it positively which is the correct way of doing it. Tony looked at it, 'he hasn't got any other problems, you know he's perfectly all right except he's deaf'. But I couldn't accept it like that. I thought 'why me? Why my child?'

Are Pat's difficulties inevitable, or those which professionals could help to avoid? The couple certainly feel Tony encountered less difficulty adjusting to the news of Christopher's hearing impairment than his wife, but then Tony wasn't subjected to 'the most disgusting conversation'.

No-one would ever say it

Some things Tony and Pat say could be seized upon by those advocating the belief that one of the psychological stages of adjustment parents go through following diagnosis is denial:

> **Tony**: to be perfectly frank I thought it would go away
> **Pat**: oh I did
> **Tony**: I wasn't ignoring it, but I kept thinking 'well he's been through all that ... it'll come back even if it's not perfect it'll come back'. But I definitely thought it would come back .. 'it's like the fact that he can't walk properly or see properly .. it must be temporary'. I wasn't like ignoring it and thinking 'well if I think it's temporary it'll go away'. I honestly thought it was temporary ... 'something's going to happen, it'll come back or some of it'll come back even if it's not perfect, we'll get round it'
> **Pat**: I felt frustrated because I couldn't accept it. I honestly believed that his hearing would come back as quick as it went. I did for a long, long time. But nobody could tell me anything different. Nobody could say to me that your son's hearing has gone and it will not come back. No-one would ever say it. I asked and asked. If they'd said to me from the word go 'I'm sorry it's gone and there is no way it will come back', then I could have accepted it and then got on with my life but nobody would tell me.

There is plenty of evidence of denial in the passages above. Interestingly, the concept of denial is sufficiently well ingrained in popular notions of the problems people have following the news that their child has an impairment, for Tony to want to distance himself from having 'the problem': 'I wasn't like ignoring it ... I honestly thought it was temporary'. Even so, both Tony and Pat clearly indicate for a long while they thought Christopher's hearing would return, and he wouldn't really be deaf.

It looks from this, as if they did have the denial problem. But if we look closely, we find their denial is based less on their individual problems of adjustment than on barriers to adjustment of other people's making. Once again barriers were socially constructed. They were not barriers resulting from their own individual psychological difficulties; they were barriers resulting from disabling practices used by professionals. Evidence of this can be found in Pat's point, 'no-one would ever say it'.

The inescapable question is 'whose denial are we facing?'. According to Pat and Tony, professionals appear at least as keen to avoid facts as parents. Professionals must have their own motivations behind apparent reluctance to give parents straight information. If, however, they are seen by parents as not giving complete, open and honest answers to their questions, then those parents will have to build their own explanations, if they are to make any sense of what is happening to their child. A diagnosis of hearing impairment, however vaguely delivered, is a much too important disclosure for parents to be content with partial explanations.

Pat and Tony then describe how denial was compounded by uncertainties left in their minds by professionals. They disclose one strategy they were forced to take, to try and establish some facts about Christopher's deafness:

> **Tony**: this Adrian ... he was actually researching into all sorts of things with children and he was going back to university, and he asked us to write to him, which we did, and let him know how he'd gone on and we mentioned that we'd been assured that he'd be perfectly OK and this was about 12 months afterwards, but that Christopher was profoundly deaf. And he wrote back and said he'd known hearing to return up to two years afterwards. He wasn't meaning probably to do any harm but even that gave us a little bit of ... well, something, definitely.

Somehow they make contact with Adrian, whose professional status is uncertain from the transcript, but who we learn 'was actually researching ... going back to university' and so whom, though possibly not yet fully qualified, was nevertheless, seen as a person with expertise who was willing to try and help. But well-intentioned information Adrian imparts is misleading and fosters false hope and reaffirmation of the possibility Christopher might not *really* be deaf. If Pat and Tony were to share this prospect with professionals, concerns would almost certainly be raised about their acceptance of Christopher's hearing impairment. But Christopher's parents did not get to the point of seeking out Adrian *because they were in denial*; they got to that point *because 'no-one would ever say it'*.

Emma's story raised similar issues. She has a suspicion that professionals may be uncomfortable in their role as disclosers of sensitive information:

> **Emma**: it was always the same ... things like, they didn't say that Sam may be deaf or that Sam could be brain damaged, nothing like that, I was never told anything and it was only they weren't happy with him, his reactions.

Euphemisms such as 'they weren't happy with him', litter recollections of what parents were told about their child's prognosis. As with Tony and Pat, however, the burden of the professional's indulgence in personal consolation falls on Emma's shoulders because she begins to dismiss the possibility of impairment:

> **Emma**: [so] I thought 'well he's only a baby, they are like that [babies] don't care do they?' [I was] desperate.

And Emma is well aware of the trap she has been led into:

> **Emma**: it's that, that always sticks in my mind; why we were never told to look out for [him being deaf]?

The temptation it seems, when professionals find themselves imparting difficult or distressing information to parents, is to treat parents as one sometimes might treat a child, and hope they will be satisfied with incomplete explanations contrived to soften the blow. Yet as we have seen before, parents cannot be so readily dismissed. Even if professionals prefer to avoid disquieting issues, parents continue to worry about them:

> **Emma**: Kevin always said that he wasn't normal, because he used to make such hideous sounds, well he didn't make any sounds he just used to 'aaaahhh' all the time and it was really loud and sometimes it would be embarrassing because he was that loud and he just wasn't babbling, but I didn't know because I'd never had any children and you just think ... you learn as you go along, don't you?

Later Emma remarks:

> **Emma**: I know a lot more now .. about things like they didn't say Sam may be deaf.

With the benefit of hindsight, Emma clearly recognised her difficulties were not of her own making, but created by the professionals she was dependent upon:

> **Emma**: when I look back, or when we all look back, we really didn't get any answers, we just got that Sam had got major complications ... and when either dad or mum asked all the questions .. [silence to indicate no reply]. It's sort of been like that ever since.

In Emma's experience, professionals are more likely to be concerned with protecting themselves than enabling deaf children and their families. As a direct consequence of this, Emma was unprepared for news of Sam's hearing impairment even at the point when she was referred to an audiology clinic:

> **Emma**: the thought hadn't even crossed my mind, that anything would be wrong with him. Well obviously I thought, well, maybe there was something wrong, and he had to be sent somewhere for further tests, but then again you kind of think, well, 'no, it won't happen to me'.

And when Emma was told of Sam's hearing impairment she found herself propelled straight into personal tragedy:

> **Emma**: when they said that he was deaf, I couldn't stop crying and I don't think it was because, the fact that he was deaf that has never bothered me, it was again 'why Sam?' you know 'why has this happened to me?' and that sort of thing.

Like Tony, who said 'I wasn't angry because he was deaf', Emma indicates it is not Sam's hearing impairment that is the major problem, but a lack of adequate explanations. And despite her continued efforts, those with responsibility to provide satisfactory explanations fail to do so:

> **Emma**: will he be normal? Will he be able to talk? How deaf is he going to be? Will he talk funny? Will he be able to learn like everybody else? Will he be dead slow? I think [particularly] how deaf he was, I found that all very mind boggling especially, and I used to ask but I still didn't understand, and I'm not asking again because I sound stupid, don't I?

More insidious than the failure of professionals to provide satisfactory explanations is the effect this has on parents. Emma simply gives up asking questions. What we find here is evidence to suggest professionals may indeed have a vested interest in creating vulnerability and thereby effectively disabling deaf children and their families.

This theme is supported further by Eleanor's recollections of how she also feels she *was never actually told*.

> **Eleanor**: they didn't actually say that *that* was the trouble. I mean, they sort of said 'oh she has a hearing loss' and this sort of thing, I suppose they were trying to be very gentle ... after all my husband is a GP and we knew the person involved personally anyway and he probably found it awful to have to tell us she was deaf and thought 'now what am I going to do?'. It was all a bit sort of difficult, but I mean it was this sort of approach 'oh a bit of a hearing loss' and 'it may well be a middle ear problem', that was the first line of attack, there wasn't a lot to say that it was, but I suppose it was one of the things ... and I suppose there was this feeling at the outset .. 'oh well this is probably just a small problem that will clear up' or 'when they put grommets in things might improve' or 'we'll do this and things might improve'.

Eleanor was actively provided with many straws to clutch at by professionals who had responsibility for helping her manage the discovery of her child's hearing impairment realistically. If clutching at straws were then to lead her, and the rest of the family, away from acceptance of Rachel's deafness, their difficulty would undeniably have been created by professionals. This problem was found time and time again in the stories of the families who took part in our study, often being described in almost exactly the same words:

> **Maureen**: they never actually told me definite, and I used to think that he could hear, but he was my first child and I was inexperienced anyway ... but to me he seemed to turn around when you came in to the room
> **Interviewer**: so were you quite surprised to find out he was deaf?
> **Maureen**: yeah .. it was a bit of a shock to the system.

Similarly,

> **Gillian**: I knew in the back of my mind there was something wrong. I went to the clinic, I spoke to the clinic doctor, she said 'yes we'll send her for the hearing tests' and at that point, if I would have been [the doctor] I would have said 'perhaps you should try speaking louder to her and see if it has any effect ... it *could* be'. And nobody did. Nobody said to me even at that stage, 'it could very well be something to do with her hearing'. Nobody said. I suspect the paediatrician in the hospital we went to see, put it down to her hearing on whatever level, but nobody said to me. Nobody. And then when they actually tell you 'yes she is deaf, she's very, very deaf, she's only got very little sense of hearing' it's a shock, because you've been avoiding that.

There seems to be a complete lack of any well-thought-out and adequately resourced practice which provides a single door through which parents finding out about their child's hearing impairment can go. A major problem is often poor co-ordination of services and limited links between service providers. As parents received fragmented and varied information, they were placed in a situation where they had to construct their own versions of what was going on. When the parents' view of their child's situation is connected with denial, professionals can choose to attribute this to their individual stage of psychological adjustment. The real roots of their denial, however, can be found in the failure of professionals to deliver a coherent and consistent picture of the child's impairment. Pat seems to have a clearer understanding about the relationship between denial and adjustment than the professionals with whom she recalls coming into contact: 'if they'd said to me from the word go ... then I could have accepted it and then got on'. The experience of denial as part of an individual parent's or family's response to the revelation that their child is deaf has little to do with the child's hearing impairment it seems, yet everything to do with the way in which professionals impart their diagnoses.

The expert mantle

Another way in which professionals can induce shock and denial, and thereby profoundly disable deaf children and their families, is by enfolding themselves in an 'expert' mantle. This is one of many possible ways of making families vulnerable through exploiting the power of professionalism. Perhaps this happens because professional training provides inadequately for making genuine, heartfelt contact with parents. Whatever the reason for such self-aggrandisement, it is extremely disabling.

Emma recalls the first occasion when she discovered Sam had meningitis:

> **Emma**: I'm just sat there thinking 'what's going on?' and the Doctor said 'well Sam's got meningitis' and I said 'what's meningitis?' and that was it. That's how I was told, you know, no explanation ... 'he's got meningitis'. And Dr .. I can't remember his name, left me there, you know, and it was the worst feeling ever ... it was just that first like feeling of not being able to get hold of anyone, and ask somebody what meningitis was.

Such is the trust and respect parents afford professionals, however, that Emma initially explained the failure to secure adequate information as down to her own lack of skills:

> **Emma**: I felt a bit inadequate really because I didn't know what to ask and I didn't really understand sometimes what answers [the doctor] was giving ... well I felt confused I suppose. I didn't know, like I say, I didn't know ... but really it's not your place to ask questions, that's how I read it. Like 'who do you think you are to ask these questions?' Like it's none of your business really, but like it was my son and I was wanting somebody to sit down and tell me in very simple English what it was and what could happen, but nobody did.

Similar remarks illustrate how parents view their own skills as a source of disempowerment, for example, Ian's step-father:

> **Graham**: you meet up with a brick wall don't you, because you can only go so far, I mean, you haven't got infinite intelligence, none of us have, have we?

Many examples of mystifying conversations linger in parents' minds and the following quotes provide further illustration of how the terminology professionals use can make parents vulnerable:

> **Maureen**: they decided to do this .. hearing test where they do it through the brain waves .. I don't know what they do ... they go in hospital .. they have anaesthetic.

The effect of imparting so little meaningful information to any parent will obviously be to jeopardise the extent to which they view their relationship with professionals as supportive. Jenny's account shows how technical terms can heighten anxiety for parents and diminish the confidence they can have in professionals:

Jenny: they say 'oh we'll send Chloe along for a brain scan'. You think 'what are they searching for? Why do they want to know this information? What information can they get from it?' and yes perhaps .. maybe ... I should have asked more at the time, but you just don't. You just sort of accept that they are doing their job and you just go along with it you know. Because it's their job, it is an everyday thing to them ... they're looking for the reasons .. to gather information to come to their conclusions, but they're not seeing us, we're just sort of a medical number – either case A or case B, but we're not. Somehow Chloe's not seen as a person [or] what you are going through.

One outcome of putting on the expert mantle, is that parents become sufficiently mystified and deflated to guarantee they stop asking questions. Davis (1993) calls this 'the crafting of good clients'.

The tests (oh, the wonderful tests)

There is ample scope for promotion of denial surrounding procedures routinely used to diagnose hearing impairment. Eleanor's description of tests undergone by her baby daughter Rachel show this:

Eleanor: at the time you had the health visitors do the hearing tests, which we did at home in this room here, and at the time there were five of us and they were building a blooming by-pass so there were lorries thundering by and Rachel failed her hearing test and the health visitor said 'Oh, it's because it's too noisy at home, we'll take her into the clinic and do it in the sound proof room and we'll try again.' And by the time all this got sorted out and a new appointment was made, she had aged quite a bit, she was quite a bit older at that stage and very aware, as they are ... and she passed it with flying colours. Although she didn't turn to the right often when the noise was on the right, and to the left when the noise was on the left, she did turn one way or the other and they said 'fine, she's passed her hearing test'. By which time she must have been about seven or eight months older. But we were beginning to be suspicious because the sort of traditional room in the house for the baby was a tiny small room and the cot was behind the door, so you had to open the door and the cot's behind it so unless the child can hear you she wouldn't even know that you were there which in a way was fortunate because we became aware that Rachel didn't know we were there. She wasn't immediately responding as we were going in ... you know, it's just one of those niggling things ... she was still quite noisy .. she made noises, she was not exhibiting any sort of strangeness really. But then we all went away on holiday and I think we just had time to think about it you know, when we had nothing else to do except be together and relax and we did all sorts of you know, silly things, like standing behind her, shouting, and she didn't respond. So when we came back we went to the doctor and said we didn't think she was hearing very well and he said 'the tests, oh, the wonderful tests don't say your daughter's deaf'.

It is easy to see how, if professionals are dismissive of diagnostic test results, then parents might also be persuaded to dispute them. So once again, we can see opportunities exist for professionals actually to induce denial. Hearing tests are uncertain affairs as Eleanor explains, and this raises a variety of practical and logistical questions about how practitioners can ensure problems surrounding testing do not become continuing ones for a family. Eleanor's experience is not particularly unique. Jenny, reported the same:

> **Jenny**: I kept thinking 'she's not responding as such'. We went to the clinic .. fortnightly, you know, and mentioned it. They gave her ... I think it was her seven-month hearing test, and passed her. So I was relieved ... [I thought] 'the experts have told me she's not deaf. She's got older sisters so they'll do things, so she'll grow out of this [it's] because they do things for her ... oh I'm just thankful you've told me she's not deaf.'

Professionals are well aware that routine methods used in screening for hearing impairment, such as the 'Distraction Test' are not always reliable and emphasis is placed on the need to utilise a variety of co-ordinated assessment strategies (Scanlon and Bamford, 1990; McCormick, 1993). They must also be well aware that hearing parents, mostly with no direct experience of hearing impairment or deaf people, may frantically be hoping for negative results. Several parents acknowledge this:

> **Jenny**: you pray .. you think 'oh yes .. please let it be. Don't let her be deaf'. You sort of cushion it from your mind. It's a sense of .. 'they're going to tell me that she's not deaf' .. you want them to tell you that.

> **Maureen**: the fact is really I was wanting a miracle.

For all of the above families, there were additional factors to signal the need for circumspection; a history of congenital impairments in Rachel's family; Chloe was known to have been deprived of oxygen at birth; and Ian was born prematurely with complications. Good practice, for these children and their families, would consist of an especially diligent programme of surveillance. Jenny went on to say this herself:

> **Jenny**: you'd have thought they'd have recalled her, because [of her oxygen deprivation] .. but 'oh no, no, no, she's passed her test'.

The challenge for professionals here, is to make sure their presentation of tests and testing does not involve them in the creation of disablement by leading parents into denial.

Taking parents seriously

Major ways in which professionals contribute to the disablement of deaf children and their families can be seen in the finding-out phase. Ironically, disablement of deaf children and their families can stem from the denial that professionals assume parents will experience, whilst they themselves appear to engage overtly in denial in the first instance, thereby ensuring its reproduction. Gillian's story of how her family discovered their daughter is deaf provides an excellent example of the tensions that arise when professionals are involved in the production of denial, often through trivialising the version of reality with which parents present them. We feel it is worth quoting Gillian's story at some length:

> **Gillian**: I knew there was something wrong and I couldn't put my finger on what it was. I know it sounds stupid and you feel really ... I mean when she was diagnosed I could have kicked myself because it was so obvious and it all fell into place... She couldn't make herself understood ... she was getting a bad name in the play-group because she used to beat up the other children out of frustration ... and I couldn't put my finger on what it was. And it was actually at my sister's wedding, one of my brother-in-law's relations said to me 'go and have Siân's ears done, for goodness sake because my daughter had glue ear bad when she was a child and Siân sounds just like Carolyn did'. I'd been badgering the health visitor to please tell me why was she getting like this, 'why are we not communicating? ... Why aren't we getting the feedback that we should be getting?' By which time .. Oliver was 12 months and was talking, this is my second one, and he was very verbal, and it was very obvious to me ... I mean it had been obvious all the way through. Simple little things like I said to the health visitor at six weeks on 'erm, how do I talk to this one? We don't seem to be getting any response when we talk to her.' ... 'Oh tell it stories', but I can remember sitting at the time in the flat, with Siân in the baby-seat, talking 'chicken-licken' to her, thinking 'this is a complete and utter waste of time. Health visitors have got no idea what they're talking about', because her face was completely blank. ... I just thought 'oh this health visitor doesn't know what she is talking about. Obviously babies don't take any notice at this age' and then I really just dismissed it. And then you just get on into your own routine and things go on, and you go on and you don't take any notice, and yet in the back of my mind I knew there was something not quite right. And I couldn't put my finger on it. Nobody in the family knew, and all our family live away so ... I was relying on the health visitor and the doctors to tell me ... And for whatever reason, the fact that [the health visitor] was Welsh and I was English, the fact that I was university educated and therefore ought to have been able to work this out for myself or whatever reason, it is actually written down in my .. in Siân's clinic file that I was neurotic and I wanted this child to be abnormal.

In Gillian's story we see how deaf children and their families can be profoundly disabled by professionals who do not take parents' concerns seriously. If professionals do have a vested interest in producing vulnerability then there is evidence they might have succeeded with Gillian's family. In addition to failing to diagnose Siân's hearing impairment, with all the ramifications of this for delayed intervention and support, professionals have made, without any substantive evidence as far as we could ascertain, a covert diagnosis labelling Gillian as 'neurotic' and recording in medical records that she 'wanted [her] child to be abnormal'. These actions are unreservedly seen as disabling.

To some extent, Gillian's situation was complicated by geographical factors. When she refers to Siân at six weeks old the family was based in a city in one corner of the country, whereas shortly after this they moved to a rural area in another. Difficulties may partly be a problem of agency boundaries, which prevented services in the different regions of the country from being adequately linked. But this alone would not account for the complete lack of support Gillian felt she needed and to which she was indeed entitled. Gillian found herself at the mercy of variations in local service provision, dependent not just on individual competencies, but on individual personalities too.

Her perception of how her concerns about Siân were taken when they first surfaced, is that they were trivialised. She conscientiously follows advice given to her by the health visitor but quickly suspects she has been misguided 'I just thought "oh this health visitor doesn't know what she is talking about" '.

Professionals are familiar with the idea that these first contacts with support and guidance services are critical in determining the subsequent nature of relationships between parents and professionals (McCormack, 1992). In Gillian's case, barriers to effective collaboration with service providers have immediately been instituted as a result of the failure of professionals to demonstrate they can offer any realistic support. What is more alarming, however, is that ultimately, professionals come to interpret their failure to provide effective support as evidence of *Gillian's failure* to engage realistically not only with them, but also with her child. The possibility that the lack of response from professionals created problems for the family is given no credence, and an assessment is made which places Gillian firmly in the role of causing the problems. We return again to the roles in which parents of deaf children are placed by others in Chapter 6.

In Gillian's story there is, however, plain evidence that problems were created because professionals insisted for so long that they had a more realistic view of Siân than her parents:

28

> **Gillian**: I'm sure that in the past I'd sort of slapped Siân because she hadn't taken notice of me, whereas [once hearing impairment was confirmed] we could say 'well of course she hasn't taken any notice, she can't hear me you silly person' ... I'm pretty angry, looking back at it,

and

> **Gillian**: the frustration [was] that you knew there was something wrong, you couldn't put your finger on it and you couldn't get the professionals to tell you what it was.

Emotional difficulties arose for Gillian, not because she is an individual with pathological neuroses, but because the professionals she depended on discounted her concerns and placed 'the problem' squarely within Gillian rather than looking for other explanations. The disabling effects of this are easy to see:

> **Gillian**: you feel very guilty actually because you didn't see it. You are her mother, you should have been able to pick it up, you should have been aware of it. You feel such a complete and utter fool that you did not see and connect with the fact that she couldn't hear.

It is nothing short of miraculous that even though Gillian discovers the fundamentally disabling views professionals not only hold of her, but also perpetuate through the system of clinical notes, she remains absolutely committed to the pursuit of effective partnerships with them. She is prepared to tackle absolutely any kind of barrier, 'the fact that [the health visitor] was Welsh and I was English, the fact that I was university educated', in order to carve out positive, collaborative relationships, but she is talking about barriers of nationality and education which surely should have no place in determining the support professionals are prepared to offer deaf children and their families.

Gillian's story provides compelling evidence for the idea that deaf children and their families may be disabled less by hearing impairment than by the professionals who supposedly enable them. The idea that the reactions and responses of other people largely determine the prognosis for deaf children and their families is corroborated. Fortunately for Gillian, Siân and the rest of the family, not everyone around them operates in such disabling ways as the professionals she describes. They finally start out on the path to having Siân's hearing impairment diagnosed thanks to the intuitiveness, not of sensitive, helpful professionals, but 'one of my brother-in-law's relations'. There are many issues for professionals and student practitioners in Gillian's account which demand sombre reflection.

Unfortunately, Gillian's experience is far from unique. Jenny also describes how she fell foul of what she calls 'the over anxious mother sort of thing .. you've been told by the experts so what's the problem?'. Earlier in this chapter we saw Chloe passed her hearing tests, but despite reassurance from professionals, Jenny remained uncertain about the accuracy of results:

> **Jenny**: a couple of months went by. It was really other people saying, you know ... and actually I used to work in a club and the stewardess at the club, her parents had been deaf .. and she used to see Chloe quite often. I used to go cleaning this club, and Chloe used to come with me you know a baby in a pram, and I said to her one day 'I'm sure Chloe's deaf' ... I said 'watch this' and I sat her on my knee with her back to me and screamed at the top of my voice .. she just carried on playing. So she said 'oh, yeah, right, come on, I'll take you down to your GP'.

But when Jenny gets as far as going back to her GP, after months of repeatedly raising concerns, her anxieties are deprecated:

> **Jenny**: he just did a few little tests, jangling keys etc., and he said 'yeah there is something, probably she'll just need grommets'. And they'd drain the fluid etc. So all the time you think .. you don't think it's as bad as what it is.

Further evidence of how professionals lead parents into denial. Unfortunately, as we have also seen before, palliatives professionals offer to parents disable, rather than enable deaf children and their families. Gillian mentions the magnitude of this problem in her personal network of families:

> **Gillian**: an awful, awful lot of mothers with babies have said to me they've had problems, and they've said 'the doctors simply don't listen. I knew my baby was such and such.' And you hear it so often you wonder what on earth these wretched doctors are doing with themselves.

Some professional groups such as those in audiology, have stressed for some time the importance of listening to parents' concerns about hearing as a diagnostic tool: 'parents' suspicions of the presence of hearing impairment in their off-spring are known to be reliable and should be used as a routine indicator in screening programmes' (McCormick, 1988). Still the message does not get through to enough.

Gillian goes on to explain how easily an unsatisfactory encounter with a professional can put parents off:

> **Gillian**: it only takes one, it only takes one doctor to be a bit off. I suppose they're brought up in such an environment, you know the best schools, and then they go to college, they've got wonderful qualifications, fantastic you know, but when it comes down to actually dealing with people, and what effect their wonderful knowledge does to people ... well you don't ever get to talk to them.

Jenny echoes Gillian's questions about the adequacy of interpersonal skills training for professionals:

> **Jenny**: they do the training obviously .. they're trained about their specific job [but] how much [about] actually dealing with emotions and feelings?

When professionals have masses of specialist knowledge but fail to share this with families in meaningful ways, we feel they are producing and maintaining vulnerability.

Recognising priorities

The next thing we would like to point to in this chapter concerns personal priorities for families at the time when diagnosis is confirmed. This issue struck us as important because it serves as a useful reminder that hearing impairment is not the only determinant in the lives of deaf children and their families. Many other things can be happening at the time when parents find out a child is deaf, which will impact very strongly on the way in which the family feels about the news. It cannot be assumed that families share the same attributes and the same needs at the time of diagnosis. Perhaps this can be most readily seen in relation to parents of children who have suffered health crises. A diagnosis of hearing impairment may not be quite the personal tragedy professionals assume. Maureen describes her feelings on being told Ian is deaf:

> **Maureen**: because he was premature, they thought he would be lucky if he got away without anything so they were keeping an extra eye on him anyway. He was only two pounds and he was lucky to survive really .. you know, after I found out he was going to survive ... you know, even if he is deaf, or whatever, I have got him. They said to me all along in the special care unit it was fifty-fifty that he would survive, but they told my husband that there wasn't much chance at all, you see, so really, once I knew that, I thought 'well at least I have got him'... you know, 'even if he is deaf, or whatever, I have got him'.

Tony's sentiments are similar:

> **Tony**: well in hospital when I realised he was deaf ... my first thought was 'well that's the least of our worries'. You know, 'he's here and he's alive and he's OK and he's going to get back on his feet'.

But it is not exclusively recent ill-health that influences the priorities of families receiving a diagnosis of hearing impairment. There are many other aspects of family life which determine the way they respond. For Eleanor's family for example, diagnosis of hearing impairment could not detract from their joy at Rachel's arrival as the first daughter, a sister for two little boys, and a live baby following a recent infant death. That professionals may not always be sufficiently mindful of the family's own priorities can be plainly seen in Eleanor's recollections:

> **Eleanor**: [the doctor was saying] 'we want to do the best for her and so we'll get her a hearing aid' which ... you know, you've got this beautiful little girl, having had two boys and having lost a little one ... to be told 'oh we'll just give her hearing aids' you know it's a bit of a shock to put it mildly.

An insightful remark made by Gillian is helpful here:

> **Gillian**: you get an awful lot of doctors who think because it's a medical condition ... 'oh it's only this and it's only that'. But it isn't 'only' that.

And it is not necessarily hugely levelling significant life events, such as those experienced by the families quoted so far, which can impact on the way in which a family reacts to the diagnosis of a child's deafness. There are many ordinary aspects of family life that may have to take precedence as Gillian's story goes on to show. We already know from passages discussed earlier, that Gillian first started to worry about Siân when she was six weeks old. The family finally obtain a diagnosis of hearing impairment on Siân's third birthday:

> **Gillian**: there I was seven-and-a-half months pregnant with my third child and I had a small baby [and] a three year old. When [the diagnosis] came [it was] her third birthday, in the middle of the afternoon. You know it was one hell of a shock. We went to see the consultant in the hospital to have the diagnosis confirmed, you know, and he has no idea about deafness, and he has no idea what it's like to have a deaf child, and there we were. I was so largely pregnant, one small baby, one three year old, two adults, completely isolated. We had heads like sieves. And afterwards, after the diagnosis, it was nothing. Blank. Mike took it very matter of factly, and I .. I suppose being pregnant was quite emotional about it initially, I was, quite upset, because I just didn't know what the future held for her. I just didn't understand, I didn't cope ... I tell you, I just switched it off. Didn't want to know. I didn't want to cope with it.

When Gillian says her immediate reaction was shock,

> **Gillian**: shock, I think. The fact that we were right and that there was something wrong,

it is easy to see that this stems not from dread of hearing impairment, but from realising the enormity of her ordeal at the hands of professionals. The diagnosis of hearing impairment itself, is in fact, far from shocking:

> **Gillian**: you feel relief that perhaps, you know, from this point it's got to get better.

Another parent, Helen, told us:

> **Helen**: I didn't break down and cry all over the place ... I didn't think 'oh my God, why has it happened to me?' I just felt right, I have a job to do and I have to do it to the best of my ability.

To professionals who believe in the inevitability of emotional problems following diagnosis of a child's hearing impairment, Helen's and Gillian's reactions, characterised as they are, by relative indifference, even comfort, might be construed as further confirmation that 'most parents' have 'difficulties, emotionally, in coming to terms with their child's deafness' (Lynas, 1994). On the basis of the evidence presented, however, we would suggest there is a more powerful case to indicate that many professionals have difficulties enabling parents in coming to terms with their child's deafness. It is not necessarily parents who have a problem.

Better support

We have now considered a range of ways in which the behaviour of professionals can impact on the manner in which parents respond to the news that their child is deaf. We have seen how the extent to which a family is launched into personal tragedy can be strongly determined by the way in which professionals present, or conversely conceal, information; who they choose to deal with; their conduct in relation to testing procedures and the account which they take of a family's wider personal affairs. With these discussions in mind, we can now look at what the families said about how professionals could help them more effectively at the point of diagnoses.

Jenny's reaction is fairly typical of those described to us and provides a useful place from which to depart:

> **Jenny**: first of all I was very angry. And frustrated, yeah ... [starts to cry] ... it's hard to explain. Those emotions never left me for a long time. They do recur still. You think you've got this perfect, healthy baby and then suddenly your world is turned upside down .. [the professionals] just expect .. because they know what route a deaf child takes they expect you to, and you don't. It's a new thing to you ... but when you've been told that [the child is deaf] and you're just left there .. just left, just with it ... there's nobody. Nobody came. But I think we needed counselling. It is a shock.

Shock is part of Jenny's reaction, but then what she remembers of being told that Chloe is deaf is, undeniably, shocking:

> **Jenny**: you are just alone, there is nobody there ... it is just like saying

'there's no beef sausages, there's only pork' but then in actual fact they are saying 'your daughter is deaf'. And you know they don't have any thought on it afterwards ... they just think you've no feeling. There was just nothing.

We have argued that a parent's anger, frustration and shock originate not from their personal difficulties with psychological adjustment to news of their child's hearing impairment, but in the main, from difficulties created through the approaches and values, training and working practices of professionals. Parents we spoke to will find this quite self-evident. They were able to offer a range of strategies for enabling professionals to cope more effectively, all of which focus on breaking down practical barriers and none of which seeks to locate the problems within individual professionals themselves. The resilience of parents in this respect is all the more impressive because the professionals they encountered, as we have seen, consistently chose to view problems as within individual children or parents.

Some of the strategies parents put forward for how professionals might better enable deaf children and their families at the point of diagnosis are presented next.

All of the parents wanted someone to whom they could talk; not necessarily hours and hours with the top expert, just contact and some very basic information:

> **Gillian**: somebody who knew, not necessarily all the ins and outs of deafness, the academic, the audiology side of it ... but just somebody who is aware ... who can just talk you through accepting. Yes, your child hasn't changed, physically they are the same child you still love them but .. your whole perception of what they are going to be changes, just like that. One minute you've a child who has got a problem you can't get your finger on, and the next minute you've got a child who is deaf and is labelled that, and you don't know what the prognosis is, what you're going to end up with at the end of the day. ... You've got your conceptions and ideas that are stuck in stereotypes and is your child going to come out like that? What are the hearing aids going to do for her? I mean nobody said to me how hearing aids work, what they were going to provide for her, how much extra hearing she was going to get with them, you just have to learn that for yourself. .. I know you've got to learn with experience but if somebody had told us at the beginning, when Siân was diagnosed. They said 'she's deaf'. I had no idea what that meant.

Laurenzi reported a similar catalogue of gaps in support following diagnosis of hearing impairment. He describes the shortcomings as 'almost unbelievable' given statutory responsibilities placed on health authorities to provide deaf children and their families with back-up (Laurenzi, 1994).

Maureen identified many of the same omissions as Gillian, and points out it is not only professionals who can provide support:

Maureen: what helps? Well, talking, if you can talk to another parent, who's got really the same problem, and really, you do need a lot of advice, I mean, from anybody you can get really, as long as they know what they're talking about.

Her husband Graham adds a pertinent reminder:

Graham: that don't mean professionals know what they're talking about, does it?

Obviously no single professional will know all the answers to every family's questions at the stage when they find out their child is deaf, and parents did not expect this. They simply wanted their concerns to be taken seriously and for professionals to try and understand their perspective. Gillian's words provide an excellent indication of how she feels professionals can take personal tragedy out of disclosure of a child's hearing impairment:

Gillian: professionals ... put yourselves in the parents' position. For goodness sake listen to me because you can't possibly know, as a professional, what it is like living and being on the receiving end unless you listen to what parents like me have got to tell you. But umm, this might be like the band wagon, banging on at professionals, but you sort of give out this diagnosis and the parent has to go away and take it all. They can't leave it because they can't forget about it, it's there for the rest of their life. And you, you can walk out of the door and forget about it. But you should always remember what effect it has on the person whose baby it is. And a lot of them don't. A lot of them aren't aware even that it has any effect really.

Summary

We have tried to show in this chapter that disabling experiences can be created around diagnosis of a child's hearing impairment. We have argued that it is convenient for professionals to view problems associated with diagnosis of hearing impairment as located within individual children and their families, rather than as a product of social and environmental barriers which they themselves may play a key role in perpetuating.

The challenge is for professionals to view oppression and not impairment as the problem. An easy way to start dismantling some of the socially constructed barriers to coping with finding out about a child's hearing impairment would seem to be for professionals to listen to what parents have to say about ways of improving practice.

DISMANTLING BARRIERS

Families – who can help you?

It is important that if we need support we know where to seek it out. To discover who can help you, make a list of *everyone* in your personal network who could possibly help you in some way, however small. You might like to make several lists, of people you know in different ways, for example: professionals, relatives, friends, neighbours, friends of friends, work colleagues, people you know socially, through interest groups, people you know through other activities such as attending clinics or school perhaps.

Different people can help you in different ways. When your network list is as long as possible, identify who can help you with what. For example,

- who can you contact for advice about your deaf child?
- who could you turn to for personal support?
- who can you contact to share some time with away from the family?
- who else can help you if, say, someone you would like help from is unavailable?
- who can help you if you don't know who to turn to on a particular thing?

Have a look over your lists and see where there are gaps in your personal support network. Who can help you to contact the right people to fill those gaps? What do you have to do to strengthen the network of support available to you? How can you keep in touch? Remember that people like to hear from others, they like to feel helpful and often feel flattered if you ask them for support and advice – if you have doubts about this, it might help to think what you would do if you were asked to give help. If you find yourself up against barriers which disable your child and family, who can help you to break those barriers down?

Professionals – who can help you?

Make a list of any changes you would like to bring about having read what parents have had to say in this chapter. Identifying others who can help you is an important step in developing personal effectiveness. Make a similar list as suggested above, of *everyone* in your personal network who could possibly help you to bring about change.

When your network list is as long as possible, identify who can help you with what. For example,

- who can you contact to share concerns you have about aspects of your work?
- who could you turn to for personal support – both at work and away from work?
- who can you contact for in-service training possibilities?
- who can help you dismantle barriers which stand in the way of change?
- who can help you if you don't know what steps to take next?

36

Have a look over your lists and see where there are gaps in your personal support network. Who can help you to contact the right people to fill those gaps? What do you have to do to strengthen the network of support available to you? How can you keep in touch? You may need to think about who holds the power in your networks, who is close to whom and what you can do to capitalise on the contacts you have.

CHAPTER 3
Getting Communication Going

Introduction

In this chapter we address those practical consequences of finding out that a child is deaf which relate to getting communication going. We continue to try and visualise ways in which the difficulties families face can be minimised by good professional practice and will analyse what parents have told us in relation to this theme. We argue that supporting a family in their choice of the right communication method for their child is potentially the most enabling contribution professionals can make to subsequent successful outcomes for deaf children and their families. On the other hand, we will present material which suggests choice of communication method provides professionals with maximum opportunity to disable deaf children and their families if they fail to act with the highest degree of personal and professional consideration.

As we saw from the previous chapter, the first step professionals can take on the road to taking oppression and disablement out of the experience of hearing impairment for deaf children and their families, is to reflect upon what parents have to say about what is, and conversely what is not, helpful to them. This equally applies when they come to tackle the problem of how to get communication going.

Once families learn their child is deaf, the issue of the development of communication emerges as one of considerable concern. It may be raised by family members themselves initially or by anxious friends or, quite likely, by professionals involved at this point. Communication is vital because it links directly to access to information, education and opportunities throughout life. In the first instance, however, it is important for families to get effective communication going, in order to provide a means of interaction at home which will enable the child to learn about the world in which they find themselves, and about the people they are surrounded by.

The way in which communication is established can have wide-ranging repercussions, not just for deaf children, but for their families and friends too. Families quickly discover, however, that the process of choosing the way to communicate is far from straightforward.

There has been a sustained argument about whether deaf children should have access to sign language or just to spoken language (Bench, 1992; Lane, 1991; Lynas, 1994). It has given rise to heated academic exchange, divisions amongst and within professions and fierce resentments, especially from Deaf adults who are members of the Deaf Community, with a right to their own language, that is, sign. The ins and outs of claims professionals make about the advantages and disadvantages of sign language and/or spoken language have been discussed at length by many writers (Fletcher, 1987; Kittel, 1991; Lynas, 1994; McCracken and Sutherland, 1991). We do not propose to make the relative merits of each language the subject of much examination here. This is because we found parents attach more urgency to the disabling effects of the controversy itself, the control of information and power professionals have over this, and attitudinal barriers families come up against when they are asked to decide upon a mode of communication. It is necessary, however, to summarise the range of communication options on offer to deaf children and their families which currently fall into three schools of thought:

1. those who feel deaf children should be encouraged to use their residual hearing with the help of appropriate amplification, and to develop spoken language as the main means of communication. This approach is often known as 'oralism'.

2. those who feel, in addition to provisions valued within an oral approach, deaf children should be given some visual and manual support to help them develop spoken language. This approach is often known as 'total communication'.

3. those who feel deaf children should be given the chance to develop both a spoken language and a signed language. This approach is often known as 'bilingualism'.

Instead of pursuing well-rehearsed arguments professionals have protracted about how successful each approach is, we will consider the issue of which communication method is best for deaf children and their families in relation to topics which parents drew on from the cutting edge of their experience.

In this chapter, we argue that there is not simply a necessity for clear, unbiased information about communication approaches, but also a need to take account of the basis upon which we all make decisions for ourselves and others in relation to the things we value in our lives. The theme of whether service providers have vested interests in producing dependence and vulnerability arises again here as we find evidence that sometimes professionals appear to put their own values first when it comes to advising about methods of communication. We have argued elsewhere that favourable assessments of the prospects of various communication methods can be obstructed by professionals who are reluctant to undertake a full and systematic appraisal of their own partiality (Moore, 1993), and during the course of this chapter will present further evidence that this is so.

Many of the parents we met talked in depth about the issue of getting communication going, and their comments will firstly illustrate their concerns over deaf children's development as communicators. Factors which influenced parents' choice of communication method will be considered and then the discussion will broaden to reflect the parents' emergent satisfaction with the decision.

Starting out

Parents watch their child grow and change at close quarters. As they watch them making the first moves towards becoming communicators, parents can delight in the start of two-way interaction. Babies will imitate facial expressions, and 'a baby's smile is a language everyone understands' (quoted in Burman, 1994). Maureen makes this point:

> **Maureen**: you don't really realise all the problems then, you're just looking at a baby that doesn't look any different .. I mean a baby doesn't even talk, does it?

Helen, reminiscing with daughter Katy, makes the same point:

> **Helen**: when you were young, you didn't seem very different from other children.

Eleanor explains how even when a deaf baby babbles there may be no outward cause for concern:

> **Eleanor**: there was a time when ... she was quite a vocal child, and in quite a pleasant way, she had quite a nice voice, she wasn't sort of gruff or grumbly or anything like that, she didn't appear to be anything different from any of the others.

When a child is deaf, however, the course communication takes after these early stages may become more problematic. Hearing parents, for example, increasingly expect to communicate through sound and speech, whereas a deaf child will continue to respond most readily to visual contact and touching. At this point, there starts to emerge what Bouvet calls 'the shared barrier of communication' and this can be equally perplexing for both parent and child (Bouvet, 1990). Often, as seen in the previous chapter, these first signs that communication is not mutually reciprocated prompt parents to seek advice about hearing in the first place. When Gillian was concerned about communication between herself and Siân, she made some close observations of what was happening:

> **Gillian**: she wasn't stringing words together, she wasn't using verbs, she'd got a big vocabulary of nouns, she could name you anything under the sun but she couldn't string words together and she was getting frustrated. She used verbal language but she couldn't make herself understood.

There is little need to reflect on the process of learning to communicate when a child is hearing:

> **Gillian**: you don't think if you've got a small baby, how they learn to speak, you just do it.

However, parents quickly recognise if their own child is suffering, along with them, the consequences of not being able to establish comfortable communication. If parents and children are not easily able to exchange messages, complications are quickly found:

> **Jenny**: you can waffle on about anything but she doesn't understand, she can't comprehend what we are saying. It is trying to get the information to give her and for her to understand it, the understanding. It is more complex than we think.

Thus, it can be seen from the comments above, and several presented in the previous chapter too, that families are acutely aware on a day-to-day basis of the consequences of communication absence or breakdown. Parents know best what needs they have as a family and are usually more highly motivated than anyone else to establish a successful approach that will bring them the rewards and enjoyment communication can offer. All of this bodes well for the business of getting communication going. We have to look, however, at serious complications which can be brought on to the scene, often by those whose role is to provide advice about the best ways to get the whole process started.

Power and professionalism

Following diagnosis of hearing impairment, hearing parents usually turn to professionals for information about ways to develop their child's communication skills. As we have already argued, the decision about which methods of communication to use is potentially the most important determinant of the child's future development and well-being. A clear, supportive approach from professionals would, of course, be most reassuring in the thick of all this. It is easy to see, however, that at such a critical point in the life of a family with a deaf child it could be a simple matter for professionals to encourage parents to go through one particular door they hold open, leaving the family unaware of the relevance of other choices. We are reminded again, of the power held by professionals and the pressing need for anyone in such a position to examine fully their beliefs and actions.

Unfortunately, our evidence suggests it is in the support of parents through decisions about methods of communication that professionals most frequently misuse their power in defence of their own preferences. They do this in several ways; by claiming more power than they actually have for example; by exploiting the responsibilities invested in them as professionals to exert pressure over parents to make up their minds in a particular way; and if all else fails, by use of covert or overt threats to entitlement and to the future success of the parents' relations with service providers. If this is how professionals actually behave then deaf children and their families are clearly disabled, rather than enabled, by those in a position to help them. It may come as a surprise to learn that all of the families who took part in this research independently described examples of professionals behaving in these disabling and oppressive ways.

The first way in which professionals can disable deaf children and their families with regard to options for communication has to do with the quality of information given. According to parents who took part in this study, information is often incomplete, sketchy and confused. It might be conferred verbally but not followed up in writing. It can be distorted by a professional's personal observations of, and reports on, the success of different approaches. It can be shaped by perceptions professionals have of the family and informal assessments they make of their suitability for particular routes. In addition, parents report receiving contradictory information and conflicting opinion from various sources. It is hardly surprising then that hearing parents suddenly deposited into the midst of such pandemonium can be very bewildered. They have mostly had little previous contact with such issues. Their vulnerability can be increased as arguments are tossed to and fro or possibly not presented at all. Some comments below are typical and clearly indicate just how susceptible parents can be at such a time:

> **Maureen**: [I didn't] know anything about deafness .. except my father was always slightly deaf, my grandfather had one hearing aid but it was no problem, it never caused any great problem so that was deafness to me.

> **Gillian**: as a parent you are very vulnerable, you have the most vulnerable status there is.

As Maureen says, parents also have their own experience, perceptions and personal resources to bring into the equation. To some parents signing will seem an impossible route as it may seem an unattainable skill or something that would be completely unacceptable in their own community. Others may find the idea of the practical management of amplification systems or emotional fear of stigma attached to hearing aids terrifying. The possibility of a cure may linger on, undenied by professionals as we saw in Chapter 2, and influence the way parents receive information about communication approaches. Any, or all, of these dilemmas can create uncertainty for parents. One source of certainty of which professionals can be assured, however, is that parents are willing to depend upon them to know best. After all, if parents did not at least start out believing this they would hardly bother meeting with professionals in the first place.

So, given that professionals are endowed with so much power and expertise, what did the families taking part in this study have to say about support they provided in relation to deciding about methods of communication? We shall split the comments in order to consider reflections on both spoken and signed language.

Reflections on oralism

In a mainly hearing society, the value placed on speech as the primary means of communication is very great indeed. The value attached to speech as the mainstream vehicle for self-expression and communication, faces families with deaf children time and time again, placing pressure on them to recognise that society may not ordinarily consider a child as having a complete and acceptable role within the community unless they speak. This sets up a complicated series of dilemmas for parents. An oralist approach grounds deaf children in a set of assumptions about equality and sameness that assign disability to them: deaf children are basically oppressed by oralism because of its very insistence on conformity and uniformity.

We feel an oralist approach unjustly sees communication as a problem within hearing-impaired children and draws on an inherently child-blaming philosophy. We also feel it is particularly easy for professionals to persuade hearing parents that oralism presents the best way forward and the reports we were given bear testimony to widespread manipulation. More oppressive, however, is the catch whereby if oralist methods do disadvantage deaf children, impede their learning and restrict access to educational achievements, then this outcome reproduces deficit views of deaf children's abilities. The importance of the method can be corroborated through its very failure to enable deaf children. We suspect resistance to difference underpins oralism and this claim is supported by what parents have told us. What evidence do we have to support these misgivings?

From the moment of diagnosis right through to early adulthood, families described the heavy expectations society, including themselves, has in relation to speaking. We recall Emma's response when Sam was diagnosed as deaf:

> **Emma**: Will he be able to talk? Will he talk funny? [Will] he be able to speak normal?

Andrew remembers when Katy was about eight-and-a-half months old, they were at the clinic soon after diagnosis and:

> **Andrew**: the audiologist said 'she will never be able to talk'.

The purpose of such remarks when made by professionals can only be to deflate parents' expectations of their child and reinforce difference. These reflections, coming as they do, very early in a family's experience as one with a deaf child, place a direct spotlight on the ability to talk being held up as a pre-requisite for full membership of society. Parents begin to experience this emphasis on speech in more painful ways too. Emma recalls the embarrassment of having to explain Sam is deaf:

> **Emma**: my mum said 'we'll take him to see Santa Claus' but I said 'no' because I'd find myself explaining to Father Christmas that he can't understand him because he can't talk because he's deaf and I thought 'why should I have to do that?'.

Ian's mum found it very painful to see other children developing their speech:

> **Maureen**: my friend who had a baby at the same time, her child was premature [too], but he wasn't deaf and I used to get awful upset when I used to see her child talking ... he was more developed.

In fact, Maureen went on to keep a careful record of her son's speech development and this itself, along with her comments about it, illustrate just how stressful it can be watching for the emergence of a skill which figures so essentially as a measure of belonging:

> **Maureen**: he was getting more words because he used to talk in like one or two words. I can't remember his age but he was a lot older than a normal child, whereas the normal child would be doing sentences he would be saying only two words. Now I could understand, and his nan and his dad, but probably no-one else could.

This passage also shows one of the possible knock-on effects of waiting for 'acceptable' speech to emerge; the child's conversational partners are few in number and this further restricts their access to information, views, attitudes and an ordinary childhood.

The value parents put on small attainments on the road to speech may reflect not only their desire to help a child become a speaking member of society, but also perhaps illustrate their own need to fulfil a role as a capable parent, a fundamental need that is easy for professionals to overlook and to which we will return in Chapter 6. For example, Jenny recounted a very special moment:

> **Jenny**: Chloe used to call me 'puppy', she couldn't say 'm'. 'm' and 'p' look the same don't they? And I remember she was like, perhaps about three before she could say 'Mummy' and I just cried and cried and cried 'my daughter can call me Mummy!' I used to get her hand and hold it there ... which makes the vibrations.

This triumphant moment may, however, be associated with rather less than enabling professionals. For example, this family was not given any information about signing in the early years and communication in the family was dependent upon quite limited skills in spoken language comprehension and use. Such narrow means can restrict the interactive style of any hearing parent and deaf child (Bouvet, 1990; Gallaway and Woll, 1994) and the disabling effects are appreciable. The absence of the word 'mummy' delayed, for what must have felt an intolerable period, the certainty of Chloe's knowledge of who Jenny was to her. We continue our analysis here, immeasurably assisted by a diary which Jenny made available to us in which she recorded Chloe's progress with oralism. Relevant entries are presented next.

JENNY'S DIARY

> This is a diary of events, happenings, and progress of our deaf little girl, Chloe. For those of you who haven't met her, she is an absolute darling. She's a caring, loving, bright little girl, who is quite normal in every other way apart from her profound deafness. As you read about her you'll see why we love her so much and I'm sure you'll love her too.
>
> 11th May
> Chloe has now been wearing aids for a week and a day. We have seen quite a change in her character. She has repeated the words 'iya' and 'bye-bye' very clearly. She has worn her aids a maximum of two-and-a-half hours at any one time. We have had a few problems as to keeping her mind off the fact that she's wearing her aids. She's also tending to ignore unless stimulated.

12th May
Today Chloe added a new word to her vocabulary, 'Bob aw!'. She happily chatted away while producing the word she had mastered.

13th May
Another good day as far as keeping her aids in, still continuing to chatter loudly. When a visual object is seen, a thing Chloe now does, is to tap the person she chooses to discuss it with.

14th May
Not a very good day. Chloe persisted to pull her ear pieces out and pull at her batteries. She's also having crying bouts.

15th May
Very much the same sort of day as yesterday. No interest in having aids in. We removed them for short periods then reintroduced them still to no avail. We persevered with the putting in and pulling out for approximately forty-five minutes. Still having temper tantrums.

16th May
Still having problems with Chloe pulling her ear pieces out. But managed to keep them in quite a lot longer, approximately four or five hours.

17th May
More problems with keeping aids in, Chloe constantly pulls each ear piece out as I put them in for half-an-hour periods.

18th May
Much the same as yesterday, she's attempting to say words that are said to her.

19th May
Chloe disappeared today for a few minutes. I found her sat on the stairs, she'd pulled her hearing aids out of their pockets, and removed the caps to turn the volume fully up till they screeched, she was quite content to sit there, listening to them.

20th May
It seems that Chloe is getting used to the idea of wearing her aids. She kept them on for two-and-a-half-hours before dinner and then two-and-a-half hours later in the day. She didn't attempt to pull them out quite as much.

21st May
Kept her aids in for longer periods of time. She's still chattering as much and as noisily. I think she's beginning to recognise her own name (marvellous).

22nd May
Great improvements yet again. Still very active, she's using far more facial expressions and more noises and sounds are being produced.

28th May
Chloe has now lapsed as far as ear pieces or aids go. She just does not want to know. As soon as I get one in place and switch her on she pulls the ear piece out. After several attempts of this and her feeling oh, so pleased with herself, I'm now trying the 'it doesn't matter to me approach' and I refuse to pay attention to her if she pulls them out. So she just toddles off to find another game to play. We still managed to keep aids in for three hours.

Chloe's achievements, such as developing use of facial expression, recognising her name, and acquiring new words should all have been available to her and Jenny much earlier, with appropriate communication advice and support, and without the tears and tantrums over hearing aids. At the time, however, focus on Chloe's speech was paramount and Jenny recounts the fear experienced by herself and Chloe's dad when they looked round schools whilst Chloe was still a toddler:

> Jenny: I thought 'oh, will my daughter ever be able to speak like them?' And you just ... you haven't a clue. They were older children than what Chloe was, but you just haven't got a clue what they'll be like, what the level of speech will be or anything.

'You haven't a clue' Jenny says, reminding us that if professionals choose to give one-sided information families are somewhat unlikely to challenge them.

There is a further disabling effect of the controversy which relates to the time scale involved in a child's development as a communicator. Typically parents who are embarked upon the oral approach are advised to encourage their child to wear their hearing aids, provide plenty of spoken input and await the emergence of speech (Clark, 1989; Lynas et al., 1987; Lynas, 1994). The introduction of hearing aids may be very traumatic for the family as we have seen at various points now, and can create additional practical and emotional pressure on the already strained communication process. Helen, Gillian and Maureen all recall problems which extend on those included elsewhere:

> Helen (to daughter Katy): when you went to get your hearing aids ... you pulled them out, closed your eyes, shouting that you didn't like them.

> Gillian: at a very young age [she] just used to pull [the hearing aids] out and then shut her eyes so if she can't see you she can't hear you, [she] rejects you totally.

> Maureen: it's very difficult trying to get a youngster to wear a hearing aid ... I remember the first time I took him out in his pushchair and we just walked up the road and he had to wear National Health hearing aids then which were little blue boxes in this denim cloth thing that looked terrible and I just used

to take him up the road and back, just to get used to it. And we used to get half way up the road and he'd pull them out and he didn't want [them].

For Eleanor, both finding hearing aids and subsequently helping Rachel to wear them were dreadful affairs, especially as things seemed to be going contrary to the advice of professionals:

> Eleanor: there followed a long traumatic time of getting hearing aids for a child that age. She was still quite a baby ... and down every alley there were people saying 'oh but they don't make hearing aids ..' and I thought 'they must make hearing aids in this country that are small' and everywhere you went it was 'oh, she's so small, we can't do it because her ears are so tiny'. And I thought 'but I've seen them in the clinic and I've seen children like her ... why is everybody telling me you can't do it for babies? You have to.'

> Eleanor: they also said .. this wonderful maxim 'if a child was benefiting from hearing aids they would wear them, and if they weren't they wouldn't' and she wouldn't wear them, and having given me this maxim they all kept saying 'well, you must try' and I kept thinking 'well, you just said that if she's getting no benefit she won't wear them'.

In addition to the ordeal which can accompany the phase of introducing hearing aids, we have already seen frustration for all concerned as a consequence of the drawn out absence of an established communication system between deaf children and their families.

That professionals can influence parents to pursue oralism with comparative ease, is understandable, however, because parents realistically see that diversity is not widely celebrated within mainstream Britain. In a situation where difference is viewed as unacceptable, 'normality' makes for a prospectively less oppressed future. Thus, if professionals go out of their way to convince parents oralism offers their child the chance to speak like most other people, parents are likely to accept this. The driving motivation behind the desire for speech is captured below:

> Gillian: with oral you can talk to a large number of people.

> Pat: my personal aim is I want him to be able to cope in the hearing world.

Whilst there is an understandable desire in parents to reduce the marginalisation of their child in society by ensuring they can speak, this well-meaning motive may not prove to be the antidote it at first sight seems. The effort to secure speech often means for example, the encouragement of other means of communication may be neglected and furthermore, many ordinary aspects of childhood have to come second to learning to speak. We have already seen how much time and effort parents needed to put in to getting children to tolerate hearing aids. The physical and emotional toll over the pre-school years can turn out to be very high:

> **Jenny**: she got to the stage where she was demanding most of my time. I just didn't have the energy because I'd got Holly on the way and I said 'yeah, let her go to school'. I wanted her to go just to get her out of my hair basically. I feel really guilty about this, but this is how I felt. When she went, I came home from the school and I thought 'what have I done?' I'd made a decision for selfish reasons because I couldn't cope any more with her, she was draining me. ... I mean any three or four year old is inquisitive enough as it is but you just don't think, you just go along you know, and answer all their questions, but it was so hard so .. and I just couldn't give her any more.

Pat conveys the equal enormity of the undertaking with a post-lingually deaf child:

> **Pat**: oh, God it was tremendous, it was a nightmare ... it was unbelievable. It was so difficult ... that's when I started to realise the difficulty in getting new things across to him and I started running round the house finding things I knew he knew the name of and then saying 'right that's not a 'b' it's a 'm'. That's not 'baking' that's 'making'. [Say it] so it sounds like 'baking', and I'd tell him to say that. I'd make him look at me and then look at that and say that and then I'd say 'm' for 'mummy' and I'd draw it in the air and he'd say 'making' and I'd make a big thing about it, jump up and down you see ... that's how we started and that's when ... I think that's when I realised that it's a lot of hard work, it's a hard slog.

Maureen describes the same constant input during Ian's pre-school years, trying to teach listening skills and encourage spoken language:

> **Maureen**: [it was] constant – 'sit down, your books', every afternoon it was. And me mum used to come up and do it as well when I used to be getting the tea ready – used to sit down with him and read and paint and all that ... but if he was the second child, I couldn't have done it I don't think. It's only because he was the first one that I was able to put that much time into him.

Maureen's point, that parents' resources are finite and not inexhaustible, is very important. There is also the possibility, paradoxically, that despite the very best endeavours of parents and others, speech will never sound 'quite right' and both the child and their family draw a wide range of negative labels because of this.

Earlier in this chapter we expressed our concern that oralism enables professionals to recycle negative images of deaf children and their families and we would argue the following outcomes go some way towards illustrating this:

> **Maureen**: Ian can talk and when you talk to him he doesn't really sound like

a deaf child
Graham: you know he's deaf
Maureen: when he has got his hearing aid out you can tell the difference then because he [can't] hear himself ... [otherwise] his rhythm is fine
Graham: yeah like my singing voice, flat and loud. Flat and loud and you can't sort of ... most people can't understand him as you say.

Pat said she was pleased with Christopher's speech but was herself taking the Stage II British Sign Language certificate as she had observed sign language helped Christopher 'get clues'. She told us:

Pat: [I said to Christopher] 'you've still got to learn a bit more, but you're very good at talking' ... he doesn't actually know he's doing odd signs.

And several years after all Jenny's unceasing hard work the fruits of oralism had still not come to bear as Chloe's younger sister revealed in a piece of writing for us:

Holly: I have got a sister who is deaf. I like playing with her but sometimes I can't understand her but I still like playing with her.

In fact, Jenny had swung completely away from agreeing with the thinking of professionals who implanted the belief that spoken language is all important:

Jenny: all I do know is I want Chloe signing.

It is worth looking at just how families are put in the position of accepting oralism without having any balanced indication of what the alternatives are. From Maureen's account it appears that whether or not parents can trust professionals to be impartial depends on where the family lives:

Maureen: [south district] audiology they believe in erm, in erm,
Graham: sign,
Maureen: signing, whereas [north district], they don't, they believe in speech.

So much for parental choice. At this point we find ourselves back with the question of why professionals might insist upon promoting a one-sided view of oralism. And it is one-sided as Maureen's understandings reveal. She remains convinced:

Maureen: if he had learnt to sign he wouldn't talk.

Pat has also picked up this belief:

Pat: if our son had just sat there and signed ... you know he wouldn't have bothered talking.

Maureen and Pat's common misapprehension is routinely put about by professionals who wish to normalise the experience of being deaf. But why? Why on earth would service providers, who are members of professional bodies and bound by respected codes of practice instil such a fearful (and unproven) possibility into the minds of parents without giving any clue that there might be a different point of view? We suspect they do it because oralism casts deaf children in a way hearing professionals find convenient for justifying their own involvement. d/Deaf people rightly view themselves as experts on sign language, but probably not on spoken language. Thus hearing professionals despite having no first-hand experience of living with deafness carve out a niche for their own involvement with deaf children by claiming spoken language is something deaf children simply have to have. When professionals insist oralism is the best method because, they argue, it helps deaf children to be 'normal', we suspect they may not reveal the real reason behind resistance to other approaches. Under the guise of 'normalisation', we suggest, a policy for oralism may enable hearing professionals to distance their 'expertise' from the experience and first-hand knowledge of d/Deaf people, and thus reaffirm their sense of their own authority.

In view of this argument, we feel deaf children and their families are potentially disabled by emphasis on oralism alone because it both precludes the involvement of Deaf adults in their education and development, and is recommended by hearing professionals who have restricted (and restrictive) ideas of what form communication should take. We feel there are many prejudices inherent in oralism which it is incumbent upon professionals to stop shoring up if they are genuinely committed to enabling, rather than disabling deaf children and their families. The above accounts, together with others we will come on to, lend persuasive support to the views outlined here. Once again we detect that it may not be in the best interests of some professionals to be too enabling of deaf children and their families.

Another vicious circle which presents itself concerns the widespread expectation amongst the general public that deaf children have 'poor speech'. Maureen sums this up:

Maureen: what you think, you just think when somebody's deaf 'well they're deaf, they can't hear nothing'
Graham: you think they're deaf and dumb I think; they can't hear and they can't talk.

We feel this image bears witness to a lack of successful communication options for deaf children over the years.

Ironically, deaf children and their families can encounter disablement if they do not have poor speech. Gillian, for example, suffers considerable difficulty because her daughter's speech is easily understood and this sets up a problem for reconciling her view of Siân's needs with the views of others. For example:

> **Gillian**: I've had parents come to me in meetings and say 'gosh, doesn't Siân speak well, she can't be ... [so deaf]'. And in the end I got to the stage where I used to carry around a piece of paper just to prove to people how deaf she was.

Like Gillian, Eleanor was on the receiving end of comments which suggested some disbelief in the severity of Rachel's hearing loss:

> **Eleanor**: she speaks very well. Some people .. say 'oh, she's great you know, [are you] sure she's deaf?' kind of thing, because she speaks very well.

There is obviously no reason why many profoundly deaf children should not have excellent spoken language. It must be noted that British Sign Language is an easily acquired language for deaf children too and can assist, rather than inhibit, the emergence of spoken language (Silo, 1994). Many families could find a bilingual approach to communication an excellent option.

It can be seen from this section that society's insistence on sameness can oblige parents to pursue ways of helping their child develop spoken language only. We have seen, however, that exclusive emphasis on establishing speech can be detrimental to deaf children and their families in a variety of ways, and even if a child does succeed in learning to speak well, this is not then the end of problems connected to living with hearing impairment. We will now look at what happens if parents try, accordingly, to pursue alternative communication methods. Having discussed our chief concerns in relation to what parents had to say about speech, we will turn to an exploration of what they had to say about sign.

Reflections on sign

We have referred to the open disagreement about the pros and cons of sign language. Arguments revolve around issues of, amongst other things, communication, language acquisition, access to education, academic achievement, identity and integration into society. The enormous array of books, research articles and discussion documents on this subject is daunting. Professionals working in the field have mostly had the opportunity to consider arguments at length and form their own views on the value they attach to sign language. This signals the advantageous position from which they seek to influence the opinion of parents. For example, Gillian talked about the wealth of knowledge one local professional had accrued, and how this influenced his opinion on methods of communication:

> **Gillian**: his son is deaf, and he trained to be a teacher of the deaf so that he could help his son. He's very oral, no I don't think he would actually come up and say 'I am oral, I'm all for this' but that was the way he wanted it with his child, he knows that it worked for his child.

Gillian also observes views of a social worker who called to see her about Siân:

> **Gillian**: it sounds awful, but they've got this stereotype in their head and even down to the social worker I'm sure has a stereotype in her head 'there is a cut off line these children who are profoundly deaf they should sign'. And it's not as simple as that, and I don't think it will ever be simple as that. ... To me it's unprofessional and it's not a personal criticism because as a person I quite like her. But I don't think it's a professional way to go about treating parents who are in a very vulnerable situation.

Both of the professionals mentioned above already have a preferred communication method in mind before they enter into discussions with Siân's parents. They are not absolutely up-front about their private biases, but neither do they trouble to conceal these from the family. They both preferentially present one-sided (but contradicting) points of view, which Gillian regards as a far from 'professional way to go about treating parents who are in a very vulnerable situation'.

Likewise, it is not only Gillian who comes across professionals who over-simplify the communication debate to suit their personal prejudice:

> **Maureen**: [north district audiology] ... they believe in speech. Only the very deaf, who *cannot* talk, they go on sign.

The examples given above illustrate how professionals can exploit their expertise to exert pressure over parents to make up their minds in a particular way. As we said before, most professionals have a chance to rehearse the presentation of their own view and are able to select examples and opinions to back their perspective, whereas most parents do not start out with such a fund of knowledge. Neither, as Jenny's diary has shown, do parents set out to behave in self-seeking ways, whereas those professionals described above may have done.

On the other hand, it is important not to forget that professionals are to some extent bound by prevailing philosophies in their work setting which may influence the approach they take enormously, especially where the reality is such that they are prevented from suggesting alternative approaches because no local provision is available. The factors which shape *opinions* are entirely understandable for individual professionals entangled in this fraught and heated controversy, but the *advice they go on to give* needs to be skilfully set apart from subsequent personal and professional prejudice. Gillian describes the likely picture which makes clear why this is so:

> **Gillian**: [after diagnosis] the parent is under a lot of pressure [and it] suddenly becomes a whole new ball game. There's a whole load of information we've got to take on board and somebody comes along who says 'your child is deaf'... There is all this Deaf culture, Deaf awareness, 'these children should use signing and they'll be able to communicate'. And I think that's taking advantage. But on the same kind of thing, [if] someone came along and said 'your child is only deaf', I mean that's the favourite phrase, 'they will be able to be oral no problem, stick a pair of hearing aids on them and away they go' that's no help either. You've got to have the information there in a logical non-biased form and I mean non-biased.

The importance of Gillian's emphasis on 'non-biased' information is clear. Emma, too, was the recipient of biased advice. Emma, whose child Sam was three at the time of our interview, explains how she and a teacher of deaf children 'sort of' talked about sign language:

> **Emma**: well she thought that was terrible. She felt that, she didn't think that ... She was surprised that we wanted to learn. And I said 'we're only doing it because if Sam decides when he gets older that he wants to look around ...' it sounds awful saying it like that, but 'if he wants to get involved with say the Deaf Society group, you know I'm his mother [and I] want to be able to communicate with his friends, if that's the way he decides to go. You don't know, he might want to work with them and then we [would] know that we are able to communicate with them'. Well, she thought that was ... not terrible, but she didn't think it was a good idea. It would make him lazy and he wouldn't learn to lip-read and he wouldn't learn to use this, that and the other. But we just felt it was another form of communication. And the guy from the National Deaf Children's Society thought that was super. He thought that it was great that we had an open view of everything and we were prepared to learn sign language.

Here, not only is there conspicuous discord between the opinion of the teacher and the long-term realism of the family but also clearly conflicting advice being presented by the professional and the voluntary sector representative involved. The professional is not only in control of the information she chooses to give and the manner in which she gives it, but is also in the position of greatest power. She can influence the nature of support provided and the nature of educational provision for Sam. This illustrates the disabling effect of the communication controversy in two ways. Firstly, despite showing an interest in exploring alternatives, the family's ideas are being dismissed on unsubstantiated pseudo-benevolent grounds; 'she didn't think it was a good idea', and unproven academic basis, 'it would make him lazy and he wouldn't learn to lip-read'. The family do not get truthful information on a topic they wish at least to consider. Secondly, the very position this professional holds may mean the family have no choice in who will support them with educational matters. This knowledge will unavoidably hinder their courage to dispute the presented view. The professional they wish to challenge could hold the key to future educational placement as the family realise:

> **Emma**: I think she's a waste of time ... but my mum says 'you shouldn't say that because Sam will probably benefit from her when he's older because she sort of goes round the schools'.

Emma has already discovered this significant professional deliberately excludes the views of other professional groups because of personal dislike or self-interest. If the professional is willing to behave with this degree of visible unprofessionalism then what might she do next, should Emma fall on the wrong side of her? All sorts of possibilities are planted in Emma's mind, for example, referring on to a professional or service Emma dislikes:

> **Emma**: [the teacher] also talked about the special school at Middlegate. Well I hope that Sam, not for any proud reason, doesn't have to go there because I'd rather he stay in a normal like environment.

Of course the professional in question may have been claiming more power than she actually has, to influence Sam's placement. But this is a chance Emma will have to take if she decides to follow a course of action she senses will provoke disapproval. Gillian's experience was outwardly a more positive one, but she too felt information was withheld:

> **Gillian**: the education chap was very positive 'she's got this sort of hearing loss' but he didn't explain to us where she fitted in to it. He just went straight ahead 'she's going to be oral, she'll be perfectly all right, just give it time'.

But how much time? How long can deaf children and their families afford to wait before language starts to get established? Alongside development as a communicator in the first few years of life, a child's cognitive, social and emotional development also proceeds rapidly (Karmiloff-Smith, 1994; Wells, 1987). A lack of parallel language development, which ordinarily provides the main medium through which children and those around them negotiate and share learning, can seriously set a child back, with subsequent effect on the whole family for a long while to come. Eleanor describes how professionals emphasise the importance of establishing shared communication early on:

> **Eleanor**: their main line was 'at the moment you must try to work on what she's got, because she does have some useful hearing and the thing is to make the best of that ... get on doing that rather than thinking of anything else'. I suppose in a way we were a bit caught up when things happened you know, hearing moulds and hearing aids and what people were saying about deaf and dumb language and thinking 'what if it doesn't work?' ... If there was something going on we had to agree with it and let them deal with it and manage it.

The advice to 'get on doing ... rather than thinking' is reminiscent of the 'professionals-know-best' line and could deprive parents of any sense of control. The final part of the quote indicates Eleanor had to concede whilst she had no concrete reason to disagree, and felt professional advice was best heeded, whilst she knew she may have had to prepare for a battle had she felt less certain of her daughter's progress. Katy's parents also portray the powerless position into which families are manoeuvred by the monopoly professionals have over the communication debate. Although they have the benefit of hindsight which enables them to recognise they 'went along' with current thinking, they realise parents of younger children may be caught up in comparable blocked alleys:

> **Andrew**: we were products of our times. So when we were young, the powerful thing was the oral methods and we went along with it but I think because [addressing Katy] you've always been really in two worlds. When you were younger, we thought 'maybe Katy will stay in the hearing world'. For some deaf children, it's different. Yeah, I think in many ways you are lucky now because you've got a foot in both worlds ... so for her looking back, she should have had the oral and manual methods
> **Helen**: we decided right at the beginning, we said if she doesn't talk maybe by the time she's about two years old we will learn another way to communicate ... but she started to talk at eighteen months which is very early for a profoundly deaf child ... [but] if I could go back to when you were a baby would I do it differently? *Yes*! I would sign straight away
> **Andrew**: and talk
> **Helen**: and talk at the same time because deaf children can learn to talk and sign.

And a little later:

> **Andrew**: when we were young, people used to say 'if deaf children sign they won't develop their speech and their language' but now the evidence ... because we know in children who have one French parent and one English parent, they learn two languages ... there have been measurements, to show the extent to which kids can progress along two pathways at the same time. You get a lot of bilingual kids these days don't you .. so you need different

kinds of communication
Helen: but they are still arguing about it. There are still families that won't teach their kids signing.

In this short exchange, there is evidence of the confusion arguments over communication have brought to one family, and they suspect, to many more. In the early years of Katy's life her parents followed the prevailing trend for oralism but would now have taken a bilingual approach. At the time, however, they trusted what professionals told them and 'went along with it'. Years later when Katy was a teenager they began to seek out support for sign language but found professionals openly obstructive:

> **Andrew**: even then ... they didn't like you to talk to the Deaf department did they?
> **Helen**: oh no.

As Andrew says, excellent prospects for bilingualism have long been established in studies of spoken languages (Baetens-Beardsmore, 1993; Baker, 1993; Cummins and Swain, 1986). Recently positive outcomes of initiatives combining spoken English and British Sign Language in a bilingual approach in mainstream schools are also emerging (Pickersgill, 1990a,b, 1991). However, it should not be forgotten that for many deaf children the situation can be complicated in other ways as in Gillian's family. Her daughter Siân's family language is spoken English whereas her school language is spoken Welsh. As Gillian points out the majority versus minority language and culture issues Siân has to contend with parallel issues raised for deaf children regarding spoken versus sign communication:

> **Gillian**: to a certain extent Welsh is .. like the sign language and the Welsh tend to be a bit defensive because they are a minority group .. my mum draws a parallel between us here, and her Asian children she's teaching in Barnsford, because she says that they are minority group ... and we are a minority group.

Siân is not acquiring sign language in addition to two spoken languages, but many deaf children are (Schmidt-Rohlfing, 1993; Meherali, 1994). A strong sign language base is often regarded as a considerable asset for these children (Meherali, 1994). Clearly the specific language and communication needs of families from different cultural and linguistic minority groups need to be a priority for professional support services to ensure appropriate provision is made for the establishment of a comfortable and effective first language in bilingual and multilingual families.

Controversy about the best approach to language and communication development continues to rage. The effects of the controversy itself, however, and the defensive positions which it impels professionals to adopt, can, as we are finding here, load an additional source of disablement on to deaf children and their families.

Enabling decision-making

Leaving aside the question of which philosophy on communication professionals aim to promote, if their approach is open, welcoming, understanding and reassuring then this can be enabling rather than disabling for families with deaf children. Helen identifies with this saying:

> **Helen**: the most important thing is being able to talk and discuss so that you understand why and why not.

This is often the approach representatives from the voluntary sector aim to take, offering a warm source of practical support and access to information. However, their sway can have equally disabling effects on families at a vulnerable time. Gillian felt strongly that voluntary agencies can turn family against family instead of uniting them in the fight for support:

> **Gillian**: I think parents aren't given unbiased information from a lot of groups ... if we are not very careful we'll end up with two camps, instead of one, battling for the rights of the kids and at the end of the day it's the children who suffer. I mean Siân has been very alienated by .. even that National Deaf Children's Society attitude to signing. Because they assume that if you sign you are more deaf and therefore more in need of their sympathy or whatever. But children like Siân have still got a problem. They still need to have their disadvantages publicised so that people can be aware that deaf hearing isn't as normal as apparently.

However, *TALK* magazine led Gillian to another voluntary group which she found a real haven in the chaos of the early days after diagnosis when local support was lacking:

> **Gillian**: we did a week with [a nation-wide oralist group] which was very helpful. I suppose we were very sympathetic to them because they were the first organisation to come out and actually give us any practical help ... they took the kids off our hands which was the first time since Siân had been born that we'd had any sort of time on our own without the kids. And they pumped us full of information, you know basic things like how to deal with hearing aids, where your child belongs, what sort of deafness you know, what an audiogram is, simple things that although we'd come into contact with them, we didn't actually know exactly what one was or where you fitted in.

Gillian recognises that where local provision proves unsatisfactory, there are dangers in taking wholeheartedly on board all that is said by whoever comes to your aid in an hour of need:

> Gillian: a lot of people take the attitude 'well, they gave me support, they're right'.

She also recognised bias even within the agency where she found most help:

> Gillian: some of it was biased towards the oral approach and they did push 'this child has got no hearing and see how well they can speak'. But it wasn't done in a blatant way, you know, 'we are right and everybody else's attitude is wrong' which I appreciated.

This highlights the unenviable situation into which families are placed in their endeavours to secure information of a practical nature. Bias seems almost inevitable with the current state of affairs regarding the best way for deaf children to communicate and the disabling effect on families can be seen all too clearly. As time progresses after diagnosis, parents become more and more aware of the underlying issues involved and recognise not only the complexities of the debate but also the standing of the various players involved. Gillian came back to this on a number of occasions:

> Gillian: to me the most important thing is getting any particular child to communicate ... but I wouldn't like to be the one who has to choose 'that child will and that child won't'. In some cases like Siân's it must be obvious for people who deal with it and there you are back to relying on professional people who have dealt with a lot of these children over the years, knowing what their job is ... but to me the most important thing is whether or not they can communicate and if sign was an aid to those children communicating ... but I must admit I've got an opinion. You know this is a politically controversial issue.

Despite suggesting choice is in the hands of professionals, Gillian does not wish to lose her own role in decision-making about her child. The conflicts she voices paint a picture of the immensely disempowering effect the communication debate continues to have upon her:

> Gillian: I am very open-minded about it ... I like to see both sides of everything. I like to see other people's point of view. Everybody's got thoughts but when it comes down to it ... I have to defend [Siân's] side of it. You have to as a parent. And I think a lot of parents can be intimidated by the Deaf, in inverted commas, cultural political correctness, without knowing ... I mean Siân is aware of signing, she can finger spell, she has on a couple of occasions expressed an interest in the teacher of the deaf that does a little sign to her as she goes through school, but she does not rely on it as some people, as the

main means of communication and she's had some quite unpleasant experiences ... she has been dismissed because she wasn't a signer ... being oral is not wrong. ... You are dismissed if you mention your child is oral. It's 'oh, dear, your child can't be deaf' ... because you are oral, you are not deaf. But to me being deaf is a matter of not having the same hearing, adequate hearing, put it that way, to be able to communicate without some assistance, be it being able to sign, be it having technology, requiring good extra hearing aids, whatever. And then dismissing a group simply because they are oral and they haven't got the adult political power behind them, I think it's unfair.

Doubtless, the prolonged and fraught debate will not subside for some considerable time and many more parents will become embroiled in its disempowering clutches. As a parent caught up in it all, Gillian reflects:

Gillian: yeah, well communication, you could go on forever about it, couldn't you? You've got to dismiss it, I'm afraid. You've got to think 'that's the way you're going in' because otherwise you could get yourself bogged down.

The value of what feels right

Whatever professionals have to say about the rights and wrongs of communication methods, parents use their own observations, resources and powerful motivation to establish communication at some level with their child. As Gillian reflects:

Gillian: when you know your child very well, you can communicate. You can anticipate what they are trying to tell you and because we have quite a close family ... on a day-to-day basis there's only us .. you do tend to pick up on vibrations.

Needless to say, there is a strong desire and necessity on the part of deaf children and their families to overcome the barriers to communication that may emerge. Where parents have experiences of other children's development, they are especially able to observe tiny details and endeavour to capitalise upon any opportunities to reduce the barrier. For example, Jenny had two daughters before Chloe and so was certain of her observations about her third child's communication needs from the start:

Jenny: when you go out, when you're pushing an ordinary hearing, a normal child shall I say ... I hate saying the 'normal', it's as if Chloe is abnormal ... erm, a child along in the street, you're conversing, all the way, you know. The baby's head might be to the back of you, you don't mind, and you say 'oh, look over there at doggy' so they're getting all this information, they associate 'ooo, that thing over there's doggy' – because you say it every time you see it – but you haven't got that with deaf [children] ... and you've got to show them *everything* for it to have any meaning. I couldn't say to Chloe 'oh yes, the kings and queens used to live in castles'. You have to show, every word, you've got to ... it's quite time consuming. You've got to be extra vigilant with her because say if you're out, say if you went for a walk and children wander in front of you ... you can shout to the others 'oh look there's a cow!' You've got to run up to her and tap her and by that time the incident's over and done with.

Gillian noticed how Siân began develop her own strategies at home to ensure she was involved:

Gillian: when she was little she used to gravitate towards male voices. I don't know why this is but whether it's the resonance ... my dad, but then he's very facially expressive as well so that may have something to do with it. She does rely heavily on lip-reading. She'd do this to you [tug chin], when she was little she used to do it a lot, you know, 'look at me'. She did get an awful lot from lip-reading.

Maureen also notices the initiative her child took to enter into communication:

Maureen: he lip reads a lot, which he taught himself.

Helen, whose daughter Katy is now in her twenties, remains adamant that communication is critical:

Helen: the most important thing ... is that [families] try anything to communicate and don't listen to professionals. Do what *you* think is best for *you*. Because you and your child won't suffer as much if you can communicate.

It is hard for families to make decisions about communication and the role of professionals, representatives from the voluntary sector and others is inestimable. Families say they need support and guidance and advice; what they do not need is coercion, dogma and prejudice. When professionals only offered Gillian oppressive backing and dictatorial support she coped with some of the tensions surrounding the communication controversy, by seeking out other parents. She advises:

Gillian: talk to people who know what they are talking about for one ... like other parents. Not necessarily take on board everything one parent says, because all children are different, every single child with exactly the same hearing is going to be a different personality.

Like individual professionals, individual families may not be able to provide all the answers, but they will speak from a position of personal experience. Helen found other parents could offer considerable support:

Helen: you're not alone anymore. And it's as simple as that really. Then you swop stories, you swop ideas and your experiences, and you hear about other families and what happens to their children, and you tell them what happens to you.

However, like professionals, parents and parent support groups also need to be viewed with an open mind:

Andrew: sometimes you get some quite intense self-help groups who almost say 'right, we're experts, and we're going to tell you what you're going to go through in the next six months ...' and that can be as restricting and as inhibiting as the doctor saying 'you will go through certain processes'.

Like Gillian, Jenny comments on how each family is different, as she realised when she tried to make contact with others:

Jenny: we went for this backing that we wanted and it just wasn't there, it wasn't there ... all they were interested in was what they were going to do, like 'we'll organise a trip out for us as parents'. Well we hadn't gone for that. We'd gone .. we wanted that back up. That is what we were searching for, to discuss with other parents. And we tried to say that but you know .. they had been through that process so 'what's it matter anymore?' sort of thing. I think people tend to forget don't they, that over time, they've time to forget, haven't they?

Thus even other parents with similar experiences can unwittingly oppress and disable deaf children and their families if they do not remain mindful of just how emotionally vulnerable parents can be, coming new to the situation, with its attendant minefield of controversies over communication.

In the middle of all this, however, as Helen reminds us, there is one critical objective:

Helen: the most important piece of help or information you can give to the family with a deaf child is ... you must learn some form of communication .. signing, signed English, whatever, anything that will help that child to understand the world around them. To understand speech .. to understand anything, it is absolutely vital for them to begin to comprehend, to understand the world first.

We decided to finish this chapter by including a few short stories which we feel illustrate Helen's message. Whatever else parents consider at the time of making a decision about methods of communication, these stories help to focus in on the central issue: somehow deaf children and their parents must be able to communicate. For professionals reading these, the stories will illustrate the critical significance recognising that academic debates may be important at one level, but at the end of the day it is imperative that advice imparted and support given *enables* and does not *disable* each individual deaf child and their family.

The vital importance of communication

Implications of barriers to communication extend way beyond convoluted academic debate. Anxiety about barriers to communication extend to every aspect of a family's life, and to the world beyond home and school. Chloe's parents experienced this in a very direct form when she became lost on a beach whilst they were all on holiday:

> **Jenny**: I said 'where's Chloe?' They said 'she came back to you an hour ago' ... all I kept thinking was 'everybody get off the beach' .. running up and down the beach, massive beach, wanting everybody just to get off. 'My daughter is missing!' .. Chloe was gone, I just didn't know had she drowned, or had she been pinched or whatever? I was hysterical ... thinking 'if she'll be panicking, she won't be able to communicate'. That was what was bothering me, that she can't tell anybody ... and thinking that she's going to be really upset, so that upset me the thought that she would be upset.

Distressing incidents such as this, in which the balance hangs on how effectively a deaf child can get their message across, were recounted by all the people we met. The parents' stories verify that communication between parents and children is such a precious thing and any disruption in the course of its development can cause untold heartache and agony. Many experiences which were deeply ingrained on the parents' memories are interesting because in all probability they will arise for many subsequent families with a deaf child. Those relating to hospital encounters are the most pertinent for our purpose here, firstly because deaf children can be in and out of hospital departments quite frequently, and secondly because they affirm the importance of effective communication by exposing just how impotent parents are, and how disabled deaf children are, without it. Gillian, for example, recalls the first time Siân went for a hearing aid mould impression:

> **Gillian**: she screamed the place down. I mean we can't explain to a two year old who hasn't got any language what they are going to do with her.

Maureen recalls the same ordeal, of not being able to let a child know what is going on, when Ian was six and had to have his tonsils out:

> **Maureen**: when we took him into hospital he had to have his hearing aid out, you know, and the staff couldn't understand why he didn't talk to them and I had to tell them 'he's deaf' ... and that was hard work in hospital. I stayed with him, you know. I would be his ears for him really. And when he didn't

have his hearing aids ... I still remember that time when he came back from that operating theatre, he was the colour of that [white paper] and he didn't have a clue what was going on. He couldn't understand what I was meaning. I feel gutted about it now. I feel that really was worse than the time when he was diagnosed as deaf ... because of the fear on his face. You know he was so scared and so frightened, you see ... but the actual fear on his face ... when you see that, it was horrid.

Katy's family recall two operations she had when she was a small child, both of which were turned into fearful occasions because of communication barriers:

Helen: they came round to give her the pre-med and she didn't understand exactly what was happening .. I'd tried already but without sign language I couldn't even remotely communicate the problem to her or what was going to happen except that she was going to be put to sleep and they were going to do something to her ears ... By the time they reached Katy, they had run out of girls' night-gowns and they had a pair of boy's blue pyjamas. And first of all she looked at those and 'I'm not putting those on' and then they said 'oh, and she'll have to take her pants off', and the idea of taking her pants off was not on. And she screamed and she had a complete hysterical fit. She bit me, she kicked me and she had to be given two pre-meds in order to calm her down enough ... and if I'd had sign language that wouldn't have happened. It just wouldn't have. [It was] just terrible, to have this child who's never, ever behaved like that before. Totally hysterical, terrified out of her wits. When we went in for the eye operation, about two years later ... she'd gone in all right ... she'd obviously closed her mind completely to what had happened the time before or she was prepared for it .. and after the operation they brought her through and without ... nobody thought of this of course, obviously no hearing aids in. And they lie her on one side, as they usually do, the side opposite from the one they operate on. And all the gunge had dripped down into her right eye and when she woke she couldn't see. And you've never heard a child scream like that. Luckily, I was lying on the bed next to her and was able to jump up and cuddle her so that she recognised my arms. I dread to think what she'd have gone through if it had been a nurse. ... [This is] what parents need to know about and what they need to be warned about. Problems can be absolutely horrendous ... and it's only now at the end of this conversation that I'm thinking that it is such an important message to parents ... that there are things that you will never be able to explain unless you've got sign language.

These stories all reflect the trauma added to ordinary events throughout the course of any childhood if there are barriers to communication.

Summary

In this chapter we highlighted the fact that communication is a central issue for families with deaf children and many aspects of daily life hinge on its early and successful establishment within the home. On finding out their child is deaf, and with comparatively little information, parents are suddenly confronted by issues about communication they may never have had reason to consider before. Some of these they will be exposed to openly by the often vehement and disabling input of others. Others, such as reflection on their own roots in a culture of spoken language and society's expectations of them as parents and individuals may never be directly discussed.

The challenge for those who wish to enable deaf children and their families in their struggle for effective communication is firstly to examine the roots of their own biases and motivations, and consider how to distance these from the advice needed by any one family at a particular time. Secondly, it is to recognise how intensely disabling to families is the current presentation of the on-going communication debate by those who hold power, and to reflect on how this state of affairs can be redressed.

In the chapter which now follows, we go on to consider the ramifications of the method of communication chosen for school life.

DISMANTLING BARRIERS

Families

List the things that come into your mind when you think about communication for your deaf child and family. List anything at all, perhaps odd words like 'conversation' or 'explaining' and ideas which come to the front of your mind, for instance 'people are embarrassed by my child's speech' or questions, such as 'how will we sing "Happy Birthday" together?' Look over your list and tick off all the things you feel confident and happy about achieving. Then look at the things that are left. Who, or what, is stopping you from feeling confident about those aspects of communication which remain on your list, troubling you? What do you need to do to tackle these things? Who can help you?

Professionals

Think about the extent to which the things families have said about communication in this chapter reflect the concerns of deaf children and their families with whom you have contact. Then list ten aspects of communication that you think are important for deaf children and their families, using your reflections as prompts. Look over your list and tick off all the things you feel confident and happy about being able to support families with. Then look at the things that are left. Who, or what, is stopping you from feeling confident about offering support for those aspects of communication which remain on your list, troubling you? What do you need to do to tackle these things? Who can help you? If possible, devise a workshop that would enable colleagues to re-examine their approach to enabling communication if they are prepared to do so.

CHAPTER 4
Education Matters

Introduction

Parents quickly discover there is no agreed opinion on the best approach to education for deaf children. As the previous chapter showed, there is a continual clash between those in essence who claim their educational methods will enable deaf children to speak and integrate with hearing people and those who feel a bilingual approach to sign and speech will facilitate inclusion of deaf children into the society of both d/Deaf people, and hearing people. It is important then, when it comes to deciding about schools, for parents to know how these debates about communication relate to education matters, and which recommendations are sensible. This is, of course, difficult to work out when professionals disagree amongst themselves.

So far we have stressed the importance of recognising the way in which a child's hearing impairment can be associated with disablement if appropriate support is not available to enable both them and their family. Arguments about the best method of communication are, as we have seen, potentially very disabling, and they are also very difficult to untangle. These arguments are closely tied up with debates about schooling, and so mode of communication reappears as a central theme in this chapter as parents talk about education.

Decisions about mode of communication have direct implications for the choice of school subsequently available to deaf children and their families, and so we feel it is absolutely critical for professionals to ensure the distance they claim from ideological bias is not illusory. In this chapter our aim is to explore the variety of tensions families say they encounter, at the points when they choose a school for their deaf child, and as they arise during the course of school life. We look at a range of concerns parents have about education for deaf children and examine ways in which oppression and disablement can be taken out of the school experience for them and their families.

We start by considering factors which influenced choice of school for the families we met. Discussion will then broaden to consider home and school relationships between parents and professionals. We go on to discuss issues of choice and control in relation to the major stakeholders: parents, professionals and deaf children themselves. Finally we examine the political under-currents in education which concern parents. The importance of removing barriers from the education of deaf children is our central theme.

Segregation

In previous chapters we suggested that sometimes the actions of professionals appear as if service providers have a vested interest in causing deaf children and their families to become more, rather than less, vulnerable and dependent on them. The same idea surfaces again in relation to the business of choosing schools. We discover from parents that what is played out in discussions about school often involves the representation of deaf children's abilities by professionals in such a way as to ensure disablement prevails. This can be seen, for example, in a classic confusion over schools that some parents are led into:

Andrew: the audiologists said Katy will never be able to talk
Helen: oh yes, never
Andrew: she will never be able to go to an ordinary school
Helen: she will have to go to a special school
Andrew: she would never go to an ordinary school.

Similarly,

Gillian: kids who have severe to profound hearing loss, wear hearing aids, go to mainstream schools .. for want of a better word are oral.

There is a major misapprehension in the above statements, which is profoundly disabling for deaf children and their families and which has been placed in parents' minds either directly, or by oversight on the part of professionals. Either way is equally unsatisfactory. The parents quoted above have been potentially misled into understanding deaf children who do not use oral methods of communication are excluded from ordinary mainstream school life. Whilst it is true that currently very few Local Education Authorities make sign language available to deaf children in mainstream settings, there is absolutely no *a priori* reason why deaf children should be denied this type of provision. There is growing evidence to suggest such provision comprises the best educational context for deaf children (Moore, 1993; Schmidt-Rohlfing, 1993). However, the accounts we gathered from parents reveal that some professionals continue to link provision of sign language with segregated schooling. It is often the case that only if parents reject what many regard as the natural language for

68

deaf children, will mainstream school be made available to them. This is both discrimination and disablement.

The dimensions of discrimination in this state of affairs would be strongly resisted if we were talking about exclusion of children who are prospective members of any other linguistic minority group. Fear of, and prejudice against, sign language is openly perpetuated, however, through its common, though erroneous, association with segregated schooling. The prevalence of this myth can be seen in the assumptions alluded to by one parent:

> **Mel**: well I mean Luke Shaw ... he seems very deaf and I met him quite a few times but I couldn't understand him, but he was still put into mainstream school, but there is a lot that felt ... [embarrassed laughter].

This parent's personal conclusion is not clear. Was it thought Luke Shaw was profoundly disabled by the lack of availability of sign language at his mainstream school? Or, more probably, that Luke Shaw ought to be in a segregated school because he couldn't speak? Resistance towards sign language in mainstream schools can be seen to have crept in to everyday understandings about how deaf children are educated. Children who hearing people 'couldn't understand' are regarded as more suited to segregated schools. We would argue this state of affairs exposes the system of segregated education as geared to facilitate the smooth running of mainstream schools rather than genuinely to best serve the interests of deaf children. Barton (1994) suggests segregated schooling is *not* about the needs of disabled children but is instead about the needs of non-disabled people, and Luke Shaw's predicament would seem to confirm this impression. Hearing people couldn't understand Luke Shaw yet 'he was *still* put into mainstream school'. There is clearly some persuasion that non-disabled people need shielding from the likes of Luke Shaw. If one of the functions of segregated schools is to get deaf children out of the way of hearing children and teachers then it becomes impossible to accept that the system of 'special' schooling is designed to enable deaf children.

When it comes to choosing schools, further support can be found for the notion that a strong motivation behind advice from professionals is to ensure the smooth running of their service, constantly constrained as they are, by limited resources (Barton, 1993). This often takes priority over and above facilitating positive choices for parents. Maureen's comments suggest the persuasions of professionals may not be prompted by the needs of deaf children and their families:

> **Maureen**: well he went to play-school and then they wanted him to start, this

is audiology when I say 'they' ... erm, at Sea Grove, where there's a teacher for the deaf. And he was only four and he needed, you know, specialist teachers ... I weren't really given a choice they just advise me all the time really that he couldn't go to Mill End [local mainstream primary] school. There wasn't a teacher of the deaf like, so the nearest one which had a teacher of the deaf was Sea Grove, so really I had to agree to that or else he would have had to have gone down to another school which was a long way away and probably would have been coming home weekends.

The decision to place Ian in a segregated school was firmly made in the minds of professionals: 'they wanted him ... at Sea Grove'. Irrespective of Maureen's reservations, professionals 'just advise me all the time really that he couldn't go to Mill End'. Professionals eventually wear Ian's parents down to their way of thinking. The effect of taking Maureen's choices away is oppressive and disabling to her as a parent because her wishes, and confidence in her own decisions, are both completely undermined.

We also discover evidence that the decision professionals insisted upon was extremely disabling for her child, and she only agreed to it in the end because the alternative she was presented with, was in her view, even more incapacitating:

> **Maureen**: he went to Sea Grove, which was quite a long day for him because he used to have a taxi to come at eight o'clock and he wouldn't get home till four, so it is a lot for a four year old. You expect an eleven year old to cope with it when everyone else is doing it, but when they're four ...
> **Graham**: and he went on his own
> **Maureen**: yeah to start with
> **Graham**: all on his own. You've got no choice. For him the choice was to go into a residential home or residential school. It would be residential around here because there ain't nothing.

According to Maureen and Graham, the priority for professionals appeared to be to restrict access to the school of their choice and insist upon their own view of appropriate placement regardless of the extent to which this was oppressive. Furthermore, professionals always hold the most powerful card, as the next account shows. Pat's first choice for Christopher after he became deaf through meningitis, was for him to return to the local mainstream primary school where he was already a pupil:

> **Pat**: he was going [back] to Westbrook school and that's it you know ... As far as I was concerned [the professionals involved] could all run and jump. He was going there with all his friends and I was walking with all my friends and my life wasn't going to change and his wasn't. And that was my attitude.

Pat was absolutely certain about her choice of school, but she does change her mind:

> **Tony**: we could have insisted that he went to Westbrook school but he wouldn't have got the support by any means. ... We discussed it with the area teacher of the deaf and the school psychologist he was very helpful, really in a nice way. And they really persuaded us to go and have a look at The Galton School so we had a look at the facilities and the unit and everything else and decided to go along with it.
>
> **Pat**: I think common sense prevailed at the end of the day. I listened to everybody and I thought 'I'm being a bit selfish here, I'm wanting my life to get back how it was and Christopher's to get back how it was and I'm not considering Christopher's needs really'
>
> **Interviewer**: when did you start to feel that?
>
> **Pat**: I think it's probably after I'd spoken to the educational psychologist, teacher of the deaf and I'd found out, probably.

There is evidence suggesting that professionals determine to win parents round to their way of seeing things: 'they really persuaded us' and they use possible threats to entitlement to guarantee this: 'we could have insisted ... but he wouldn't have got the support'. It does seem the priority for professionals, whether at a conscious or subconscious level, is to facilitate the untroubled running of their service even if this is oppressive. In the end they persuade Pat to see herself as the problem, rather than them: 'I listened to everybody and I thought "I'm being a bit selfish here" ' and she is obliged to accept their view of what is best for her child.

We have already seen damage inflicted upon deaf children and their families when professionals insist they have a more realistic view of a child than the child's own parents. We saw this in relation to finding out a child is deaf and in relation to deciding methods of communication. The same problem arises again in relation to decisions about school. The disabling effects of professionals who disregard the views and wishes of parents can be much more problematic than a child's hearing impairment alone.

However, choice of school is not just linked to resources. It is also linked to much wider issues to do with the kind of place envisaged for deaf children in society. Not surprisingly, in relation to this, parents we met expressed a variety of misgivings about the prospect of segregated schools; they wanted themselves and their child to feel included in ordinary everyday society.

Andrew describes his feeling of being cast as an outsider on being told Katy would 'never be able to go to an ordinary school':

> **Andrew**: you feel labelled and isolated.

Emma had similar reservations about segregated school for Sam:

> **Emma**: I'd rather he stay in a normal like environment.

Emma echoes the view of many who feel, often as a result of personal experience, that segregation teaches deaf children they are, in critical ways, outsiders (Foster, 1989). Andrew develops the point with a thought typical of many made by parents interviewed:

> **Andrew**: it's the old debate, do you have specialist education or not? Sometimes special education is good and sometimes it takes you away from other people.

Jenny has direct experience of the pros and cons of segregated education as Chloe, against her parents' better judgement, currently attends a segregated school:

> **Jenny**: I just hope that she continues to be a member of the normal community although she does go to a school solely for the deaf at the moment. In some ways it has its draw-backs, that's why we wanted her to go to the unit initially, because she would be mixing with hearing people and she would get used to it. The more that hearing people get used to having handicapped people, disabled people, within their circle then there aren't the stigma that is attached to them.
> **Interviewer**: so ideally would you have liked her to go to the same school as [her older sisters]?
> **Jenny**: yeah, I would have done. I know she can't go ... I know she can't go, but yeah, because having said the child is to be normal there are things that ... don't allow that to happen.

A major source of disablement associated with segregated schools in the minds of parents, is the role they play in reproducing negative images of difference. In addition, disablement may be created by insistence on sameness that doesn't exist:

> **Gillian**: I mean, my Siân's peer group is with other children of the estate. She doesn't even like .. necessarily have anything in common with another little girl called Sue at group meetings, Siân's age, and she's deaf and that's the only thing that she and Siân have got in common. And Siân would far rather play with one of the other little girl's sisters, or one of the other children who comes there, because [she and Sue] haven't got anything other than deafness in common.

As feelings run high at the time when decisions come to be made about school, parents may be very vulnerable if professionals choose to impose their own view of what form educational provision will take.

Again we are greatly assisted in our analysis here, by access to Jenny's

diary. Relevant entries provide a running account of how Jenny's family
was supported through the process of choosing schools.

JENNY'S DIARY

24th May
Mrs Wilson came. We discussed our visits to the schools for the deaf. We
have now arranged appointments to visit the schools.

3rd July
Yesterday we went to visit Elmhurst, and I must say we both feel a lot more
relaxed about the whole idea of Chloe going away to school. It wasn't like
we'd both visualised, some sort of institution. Our first impressions were 'a
very magnificent impressive school'.
Miss Craven, the headmistress, was very warm and friendly. She reminded
me of a doting mother hen carefully checking her brood and I don't mean to
sound in the least bit nasty. I liked her.

12th July
Went to Queen's School, on Wednesday. This is another beautiful school, we
had a more thorough look at this, we saw all recreation amenities etc. The
headmaster seems a very nice man. He fell for Chloe's charm and personality. I can honestly say I feel more relaxed about Chloe going to either of these
schools, although Doug seemed to prefer this one, yet I the other, but our visits where short, and I think at least another to each is vital.

10th October
We went to see the schools last week, this was our second visit. It's made it
harder for me to decide which one I'd like Chloe to attend. I just hope there's
no pressure on us to give a decision. I'm hoping that as Chloe develops, we
will be given recommendations as to which school it is felt Chloe would best
benefit from.

It is worth noticing the extent to which Jenny and Doug are prepared to
trust professionals. Though wary of undue pressure, they feel professionals are best equipped to provide firm 'recommendations as to which
school it is felt Chloe would best benefit from'. They value their own role
in the decision-making process but expect professionals to sort things
out, knowing they have the power and the connections to do so. However, in retrospect Jenny and Doug find their optimism and trust misplaced.
Looking back, they feel they were not given real choices, and suspect
they were misinformed:

> **Jenny**: there was no choice, that was it .. it was Prestgate or Elmhurst and
> there was no way I wanted her to go away. I could not cope with that. I
> couldn't cope with sending her away and becoming .. I don't know, not a part
> of the family ... and so she went to Queen's School which wasn't a signing

school at the time, but she started there and would go while she was sixteen. Now we'd heard rumours that the school was shutting and we put this to [the education adviser who said] 'oh no, no, nothing like that', which it did. It shut after she'd been there three years.

Jenny and Doug realised the far-reaching consequences of the decision they had originally been guided into:

Jenny: they found this other school for Chloe, still in Prestgate, and all the children come from all over [the county]. She hasn't got any deaf friends in the area. She can't even go to Elmhurst now if I wanted her to because they sign at Queen's School and Elmhurst won't take signing children.

As Jenny's story unfolds, we find she is now resolutely critical of the professionals of whom she once had high hopes and challenges their professionalism at every turn:

Jenny: when she leaves next year, she has to go to the high school across the road with a deaf unit. Now Chloe was *too deaf* to go to a unit when we asked. There's a unit at Blackfield. But suddenly, because it suits them, you see .. these things really annoy you .. to think she could have gone to a unit in Blackfield and met Blackfield people she would have had a closer circuit of friends. Now suddenly because it suits them, she is going to go to this deaf unit. There is no alternative for her. We've asked. Last time I went to the school it was to Chloe's review and the psychologist sits in every so often and he's from Blackfield, and I asked him about .. St George's here in Blackfield, it's a high school with a deaf unit 'why can't she go to this one here in Blackfield as opposed to the one in Prestgate?' 'They can't cope with that loss of hearing with these deaf children'. But they're all over the board, because the school she goes to .. Chloe is the deafest child in the school and there's some that have only got partial hearing loss that will go to that unit because there's nothing else for them. It's just ... I think they want to keep their figures nice. It's so unfair. It's really frustrating that they said she *couldn't* go to a unit, and now she *has* to go to a unit because there's no alternative. It's just not cost-worthy. You know, they've got to base them in one area and travel to them .. I understand and respect that, but it's annoying to think that if she can go to a unit, then she could have gone to the one that's ten minutes down the road, whereas she was going to school when she was under four years old at twenty past seven and not getting home until five o'clock.

As Jenny rightly assumes when she says 'I think they want to keep their figures nice', falling rolls present a serious problem for a school. In a situation where there is a threat of closure or redundancy, continued survival of a school may well take precedence over the preferences of parents when decisions are made about who is placed where. Riseborough (1993) notes that the pressures professionals face in such circumstances often militate against the interests of hearing-impaired children. Maureen also suspects the system operates in ways which are not justified by children's best interests:

> **Maureen**: you see you seem to find out after, when it's too late, that you had an option. But you weren't told that at the time ... it comes out too late.

Arguments against segregated provision are complicated, but so far in this chapter parents have identified a major specific problem; segregation reinforces difference and nurtures ignorance. Nevertheless, there are several arguments professionals can put forward to draw parents in to selecting segregated provision. For example, Ian's mother is told only segregated settings provide specialist staff and the type of education he 'needed'. Jenny is talked into accepting that financial efficiency necessitates specialist centres; 'I understand and respect that'. Perhaps the most revealing comment about segregated schools though is Jenny's observation 'having said the child is to be normal there are things that ... don't allow that to happen'. Families quoted describe a process whereby they are coerced into selecting the less segregated of two segregated school options, in the hope that this will enable their child to be 'as normal as possible'. What parents want, however, is a much more ordinary option: for their child to go to school 'with all his friends' (Pat), 'not to be put like in a separate group' (Emma), and as Tony summarises:

> **Tony**: all we want really is just for him to be an ordinary person in the big, wide world.

Integration and inclusion

Let us leave aside the disadvantages of segregated schools at this point and look at the alternative of integration. Some parents feel professionals may lean towards integration:

> **Maureen**: I think it seems in [this area] if they can get them in to mainstream school that is what they want .. and you get the kids that are deafer than Ian [in mainstream schools] and they can't speak.

Maureen then explains how, despite her personal reservations, professionals make sure she does accept integrated schooling for Ian:

> **Maureen**: you see when you're told about your child going into mainstream school you're not told about all these reactions that you will get. You're just told .. like [the audiologist] said, 'oh he's doing well, he'll be able to cope in a mainstream school' and you get that and you think 'oh great, that'll be lovely'. But when they start it you gradually see these things ... that let them down.

Her husband feels professionals withhold information as part of their exercise of power over the choices parents make:

> **Graham**: they knew all these things [problems] were going to happen anyway because they've got the experience of five thousand other children they've pushed through schools and they know what the hardness is but they don't tell you about it.

And whilst integrated education is vital if deaf children are to have the chance of an included identity, it is not, as many families know, all plain sailing. Pat and Tony, who finally obtained a place in a mainstream school for Christopher ('well it's an ordinary school with a unit inside it'), discovered a range of provisions fall within the rubric of integration and deaf children can be isolated in mainstream settings. The relevant extract from their story is presented next and then commented upon.

> **Tony**: we had a problem ... came to the third year and he had a teacher who appeared on the surface to be OK but really [Christopher] spent more and more time .. [segregated]. The whole idea of him going there, and written into his statement, was integration you see ... he spent more and more time in the unit. And we weren't too happy about it ...
>
> **Pat**: he wasn't totally happy, was he?
>
> **Tony**: no. It was a case of 'oh he's been very clever today, he's put pencils away for me' and things like that. So we wrote this letter, very, very nicely. We had a meeting so they assured us then, that the teacher, she was sat there, she was going to go Green Street and join in meetings and seek advice and do this and do that. So we thought 'wonderful'. So we all said 'no hard feelings, hope that next year will be a better year'. We stressed that we thought he'd had the best of attention in the unit, we weren't disputing that at all. The following year
>
> **Pat**: his behaviour started altering
>
> **Tony**: his behaviour started to change and he never mentioned his class teacher
>
> **Pat**: he never said what he'd been doing
>
> **Tony**: it was more and more the unit, the unit all the time
>
> **Pat**: he never discussed what work he'd done
>
> **Tony**: he wasn't very happy at all
>
> **Pat**: didn't want to go to school really, did he?
>
> **Tony**: luckily Pat goes to school with him every day. Pat spotted a few things. So it came to the crunch ..
>
> **Pat**: I walked in early, got there early one day, I walked into the main entrance and all his class were in the hall facing me and Christopher was sat there on a pile of chairs reading a comic. And they were all practising for a play in the morning assembly. The whole class were taking part and Christopher was sat on a pile of chairs. So that did it, I just stormed in and I got hold of him and the teacher of the deaf came round the corner and she said 'what's

to do?' And I said 'that's it'. As far as I was concerned he wasn't going back, you know. I mean, you know, I'd just had enough. But he'd wasted so much time. He was unhappy. But these are the things that you face because if I hadn't been going with him, and we hadn't observed his behaviour, and put two and two together, what would have happened? He would have been classed as perhaps with a behaviour problem or something like this. You don't know. And you know we had to cause an awful stink, didn't we?

Tony: well, he was never going again, was he?

Pat: Tony's a bit more sensible than me. I mean I just wasn't taking him back

Tony: I said 'they can't get away with this, some other poor child will follow along and exactly the same thing will happen' so we got stuck in. ... So, after what we'd been assured after the first time, after doing things nicely, writing a letter nicely, I wrote a letter to the headmaster with a copy to the Director of Education at [county], the Director of Education at [the neighbouring county],

Pat: everyone but the chief pope I think

Tony: [the Director of Education] he's retired now, he said 'you do realise what you could have done?' He said 'you could have closed this unit', so I said 'yes that's right. It's not working properly.' Well, he started then. He had Mr Harrington in, who was his teacher the following year, and he's absolutely brilliant

Pat: he did everything he could

Tony: he shaved his beard short so he could get his lip pattern ... he doesn't mess about. He's a fairly strict teacher but

Pat: but within two or three weeks

Tony: he was a different lad. He comes out of school happy

Pat: he loves school. Mr Harrington gave him a part in the next play, quite a major part. And he thoroughly enjoyed dressing up for it, sorting his clothes out, practising. There must be lots of others [parents] that don't know what's going on with the children really ... at the end of the day it depends on the teacher's attitude, doesn't it?

Tony: the set up, the way it all looks, if you went in as a visitor and looked round, it looks brilliant. And the years it's worked, it's been brilliant, but it's all down to them, the teacher of the class, whether they accept deaf children or not.

This exchange typifies two different types of integration. There is integration in which deaf children are nominally placed alongside their hearing peers and receive an inferior education characterised by low teacher expectations: 'oh he's been very clever today, he's put pencils away for me'. As Pat and Tony notice, this model of integration subsequently fosters passivity and low self-esteem: 'his behaviour started to change' and 'he wasn't very happy at all'. Alternatively, there is integration which secures inclusion of deaf children in the mainstream classroom, providing full access to a wide curriculum, breaking down stereotypes and ignorance and heightening a deaf child's developing sense of self-esteem. As Pat and Tony say, the advantages of the latter type of integration are tangible. Within weeks: '[Christopher] was a different lad. He comes out of school happy.' The relative merits of inclusion are clearly shown in Pat and Tony's account.

As Pat points out, however, it is difficult to assign blame for Christopher's exclusion in a so-called integrated setting to lack of professional training or expertise:

> Pat: I don't think I can ever get over that, that responsible grown-ups could actually treat a child in such isolation. I can't honestly accept that somebody in as responsible a position as a teacher could actually do that. I mean that doesn't come through education. Nobody actually teaches you that. You don't go to university to actually involve a child in something. I mean that is within, isn't it? That's normal behaviour to me.

From what Pat and Tony say, it seems that at the centre of controversies about integration versus segregation lie fundamental differences in the way professionals view hearing-impaired children, the assumptions they make about deaf children as learners and the contribution they can make to school life. As Pat points out, teaching practices can easily disable, or enable, a child. Christopher started his career at the school as a hearing-impaired child, but could easily 'have been classed as perhaps with a behaviour problem'. The problems, however, would not stem from having impaired hearing, but from an unsatisfactory school environment and discriminatory teaching.

The comments Pat and Tony make about action they took to try to minimise Christopher's experience of disablement help to develop these points. They reveal that not only can professionals disable deaf children in educational settings, but they often disempower parents too. This is discussed next.

Home–school relations

Tony, as we have seen, is most anxious to stress the care taken to sustain good relations with professionals: 'we wrote this letter, very, very nicely', 'we all said "no hard feelings" '. These efforts appear beneficial as Pat and Tony do secure their desired outcome of more effective integration for Christopher. However, further remarks reveal the power parents have to complain or ask for different types of support for deaf children, is strictly limited:

> Interviewer: so you're happier now?
> Pat: yeah. But they know how we are. They know that I'm in there. I feel I'm a pest sometimes you know

Tony: we've never gone on about anything petty
Pat: oh no, it's always been, like his reading wasn't coming on, I've been in and in and I've battled and battled and I've said 'no, he should be better than this' and what have you. I'm always feeling that I've got to battle for him. At school they're probably fed up [with me] but I can't ever settle now with that teacher there. I can't. I'm always on my guard as to what Christopher comes home and says. I never put anything in his mind but she obviously does take it out on him a bit, although she has very little to do with him and he's noticed it himself, without me saying anything.

A problem derives from Pat and Tony's decision to '[get] stuck in'. Any expectation of professionalism is suspended; parents are positioned as problems – for wanting to be partners – and their child is made vulnerable, to perhaps subconscious, but even so, strong messages that their parents are a nuisance. Pat and Tony incur all this displeasure because they simply refuse to stand by and watch their child suffer. Concerns attributed to the incredulous former Director of Education, 'you do realise ... you could have closed this unit', are obviously small fry to Pat and Tony, whose child's education and development were at stake. But as other parents also explained, if parents need to criticise or question professionals about any aspect of their child's education they have to tread very carefully indeed:

Gillian: you can't jump up and down, you've got to be a bit more diplomatic. There's a fine line between getting people on your side and ... [sentence unfinished]

For deaf children, however, open and honest links between parents and school may be even more crucial than for their hearing peers. Gillian and Pat both spell this out:

Gillian: I'm not one of these parents who rushes in at every slightest opportunity but I have made a point of making a relationship with the teacher [and] with the headmaster in the school so that Siân knows that if she comes to me and says 'look something is not right', I will go in and be her mouth piece if you like because it's a different relationship.

Similarly, Pat:

Pat: more than probably the parents of a hearing child ... there are certain things that we've got to be aware of, more aware, and we've probably got to battle for him a bit more than we would normally. But we've got to be careful that we don't overstep the mark. We don't want him to think that we're going to jump in and sort everything out for him. We've got to give him his independence but I still think we've got to keep our eye on his educational needs for quite some time. Until he's able to himself.

Several parents reflected upon the ways that practical links could be made between school and home and also explained some of the problems that arise. Consider the incident recalled by Pat:

> **Pat**: [one day] I went in and they all came out with red noses on. You know, Red Nose Day. I never got the letters did I? They'd all took 50p in and I knew nothing about it and I'd been in three or four times to talk to somebody [because] I never received letters. It was more important for me to receive letters because Christopher couldn't pick up from other children what was going on. And I stormed in again and she said 'oh there are some left', I said 'just forget it' and I stormed out with him.

Of course, it is impractical to expect teachers to improve practice or increase levels of contact with parents without appropriate support which particularly takes into account pressure on their time. The level of commitment required in respect of the above incidents, however, does illustrate there are numerous small initiatives individual staff could, and hopefully many already do, take towards improving matters.

The Red Nose Day episode mentioned above is damaging for Christopher because it makes him an outsider. It also wreaks havoc for Pat's relations with school staff, which we have already seen, need to be sustained *on the professional's terms* if Christopher's education is not to be placed in jeopardy. Another parent, Gillian, recognises the importance of communications between home and school but struggles with the difficulty of not making her child stand out:

> **Gillian**: we did get feedback just 'perhaps she ought to concentrate on this ...' you know, 'just be aware that we've been doing this in school'. We did find it frustrating, there were good intentions like we intended having a book so they could write messages, but in the end it didn't happen. In the end I suppose it made her more like everybody else, because she didn't have to fetch this wretched book home [laughs]. She could fetch stories home for me herself. ... It took a long time.

If deaf children are to have equal access to equal opportunities in school, optimum parental involvement is required, but this is not easy to establish. Gillian explains how parents have to learn to tolerate the arguments and feelings of professionals:

> **Gillian**: the sort of relationship you've got to build up .. you've not got to be critical, you've just got to be aware it's a very careful line between being aggressively defensive with your child and being sympathetic to [the professional's] point of view, and if you get, you know, 'my child must have this and should have that', you aren't going to get anywhere with people.

It is not always easy to be this rational, however. Freeman (1988) discusses the predicament in which if parents are felt to be demanding preferential consideration for their child, professionals do not like it. Yet those same professionals in their own role as parents would, of course, do the same. Both Graham and Jenny refer to the inevitable dilemma whereby professionals need to consider many children, but families need to promote the interests of their own:

> **Graham**: one of the arguments they used against our argument for giving him more time ... they had two more children coming in so they had to cut Ian's time down to give them two children more time.

> **Jenny**: my child to me is my only one .. I'm not blaming the school, they are dealing with more than one deaf child [but] I've only got Chloe.

There is also a risky course to be navigated between having close links with the school yet at the same time leaving a child their own independence. This came to the fore in parents' accounts of how they dealt with bullying. Several parents mentioned bullying as a significant school-related concern and so we will elaborate on this next.

There's always been bullying, hasn't there?

Emma worried about bullying long before Sam was due to start school:

> **Emma**: I think what will happen when he goes to school, because kids are cruel.

Gillian gave some justification for Emma's concerns:

> **Gillian**: [Siân] does get upset if the children dig in .. when she first started at school the children they ganged up.

Maureen and Graham discussed bullying from distressing first-hand experience:

> **Maureen**: you get these nasty boys you know and you get the bullying and that .. that's you know ... painful really, for him and us as well. Well they set him back. You're so pleased that he's progressing and then something happens which upsets him and then he won't go to school for a week and you wonder what on earth's happened and all he's doing is worrying about what's happened.

Bullying is the main problem Ian encounters at school and prompts his mum to wonder if he wouldn't be better off at a segregated school:

> **Maureen**: problems with bullying ... he gets called 'deafo' and all sorts you can imagine ... I think he has got a bit thick skinned about it now, and he probably doesn't hear it all anyway, it is very hard for him to go to, I think, a

normal school ... if he was with deaf kids all the time life would be much easier for him.

When we look at Ian's experience of bullying, however, we find although
it occurs in the context of integration, it stems directly from a lack of
school policy. Disablement is created because professionals fail to
address the existence of bullying and its effects. This becomes clear if we
examine the detail:

> **Maureen**: there's lots of time, lots of times you feel lost and you think 'well
> what do I do about this one?'
> **Graham**: well, we had it with the bullying, didn't we? I mean we couldn't
> ask anybody, who could tell you anything... What we did .. try, ... we thought
> we would do it the proper way which is what you'd do with a normal child, is
> tell the school .. and that was a brick wall. ... Tell them about the first time.
> **Maureen**: you mean when they had him in the office with the others? You
> see Ian, if he went into the office he wouldn't be able to say a lot because he'd
> be scared and er .. how the actual bullying finished really was er ... , the
> woman who was sorting out said 'well I've had them all in my office and they
> shook hands on it and they're all friends now'.
> **Graham**: yeah, there was two lots of bullying. The first one, was when he
> was at school, in the school playground, that was the first bullying, and he
> made himself ill, didn't he? Wanted to stop at home. He .. made himself sick
> to stop at home so he wouldn't go you see, well that took me nearly four
> weeks to sort out. That was just getting it out of Ian. He came home ... not
> very happy, he just didn't look happy, wouldn't say anything you know, just
> disappeared straight in to his bedroom. Didn't say 'hello Mum, hello Gra-
> ham' and then on the Sunday he started to be sick ... he was ill, he was. And it
> went on for about four weeks and we couldn't get it out of him. Slowly we got
> it out of him, but it was Maureen, me, his Dad, Nan, Auntie Joan, everybody
> had to have a little chat with him, but Maureen gets most of it because she
> will sit down and talk to him ... But the school .. in the end we told the school
> about it. They just said 'well the lad's going to Australia', it didn't matter.
> That was the first one. The second one was two lads, one of them wanted
> Ian's snack ... we knew something was wrong on the Monday evening when
> he came home, he wasn't himself again, quiet, just shutting himself away
> really. And then he was hiding. He tried not to go to school on the Tuesday.
> He went anyway, because he got ticked off .. we said 'well if you're not going
> to tell us what's wrong then we'll make you go to school' and then maybe he
> will tell us .. we'd tried millions of other ways and he dried his face, and he
> went to school. And he come home on the Tuesday night and he was the
> same. Wednesday night, Thursday night was the same, and then I think it was
> .. on the [Friday] morning Maureen heard some money in his pocket rattling
> ... and she asked him what it was and he said that a lad had said he wanted 50p
> off him otherwise they were going to thump him .. he was getting bullied, this
> lad wanted 50p and the other lad had nicked his snack off him on the Monday

and Tuesday and other days, but he wouldn't tell me. I think it's worse, not because he is deaf, but there's always been bullying, hasn't there? I don't know about deaf ..

Maureen: but it's another thing to get at ..

Graham: yeah, it is something else to have a knock at ... but you see the bullying carries on because those in authority, the school, the teachers don't do anything about it.

Maureen: remember that time when, erm, that woman, I can't remember her name now, was trying to sort it out and she said that Ian got it all wrong, all wrong?

Graham: that's another thing, they believe other children against Ian, don't they?

Maureen: yeah. She said that Ian must have got it wrong. Now you see nobody would have said that about a normal child, would they? Who would say they got it wrong if they could hear right? That really got to me, that really hurt me.

Graham: he didn't get anything wrong

Maureen: no

Graham: he didn't

Maureen: because I mean we sit down with him and we take a lot of time with him, and ask him every detail, the ins and outs of everything to make sure that he hasn't go it wrong because you know Ian might only have to miss one word and he will get it wrong. So I've got to sit down with him for ages and make sure that he hasn't got that problem. If I know that he's got a problem, I've got to know that he's got one, that's the hardest bit.

This extract suggests bullying goes on because there is no practical help available and no school policy to deal with it. Graham corroborates this: 'bullying carries on because those in authority, the school, the teachers don't do anything about it'. Keise (1993) points out that children who are bullied are denied access to learning in the safe environment to which they are legally entitled. Further, as Keise also notes, the National Curriculum is an entitlement curriculum yet the effects of bullying make this meaningless for Ian who is too terrified to attend school. We feel the role of professionals suggested by this particular account is to provide a coherent whole-school approach which acknowledges bullying is an equal opportunities issue and re-examines the school's response to this issue. Bullying is a major concern about school voiced by parents who took part in this study, but as Maureen points out, it is not exclusively the problem of deaf children:

> **Maureen**: there's been a lot of bullying of other kids on the bus, but I thought well 'I've got two on the bus, I'm going to do something about it'.

However, as Maureen also says, being deaf is 'another thing to get at'. The problem is compounded for hearing-impaired children if teachers mistrust their concerns: 'who would say they got it wrong if they could hear right?'. Staff may need to examine why bullying arises in their school, and how this impacts on deaf children. A range of strategies needs to be devised that could be used to minimise the problem. A typical everyday incident which would provide focus for staff reflection has, for example, been spotted by Pat:

> Pat: I had to stand with him and the teacher would blow the whistle .. [and say] 'all those that can hear me'.. this is a school with a hearing-impaired unit .. 'all those who can hear me put your hands up'. Of course, they'd all look at Christopher. I thought 'the stupid woman'.

Considerable headway could be made to reduce the extent to which deaf children stand out from their hearing peers in unnecessary ways through developing awareness.

Inclusion seems to offer the crucial key for enablement in Eleanor's experience:

> Eleanor: Rachel has been very lucky she's had children all the way from play-group that she's mixed with, who all know her and accept her as she is. She's not a freak and hearing aids aren't strange .. so she's had very few [bullying] incidents.

Thus, we can see that integrated education actually reduces the risk of deaf children being bullied. Another set of disabling barriers surround experiences when the need to change school or alter educational support arises. Again the problem of different perspectives between families and professionals can be distinctly seen in the exercise of power over choice of provision for deaf children.

Changing schools or provision

As when choosing first school, parents can be very vulnerable if professionals wish to persuade them in particular ways when the issue of deciding upon changes in provision arises. Transition from primary to secondary school can be a stressful time for deaf children and their families. A child may just have settled in to their primary school, when the question of 'where to next?' arises. There is an added dimension to the problem of choosing schools at this point, because by now parents thought children should play an active role in decision-making too.

Pat describes some of the stresses involved:

> Pat: I'm a bit worried really about him going to senior school. Because I'm going [to the junior school] every day, I know everything that's going on and

I know everybody.. I'll feel a bit detached really so I mean that's part of his independence anyway and that's a natural course to take but .. I think I've got to watch his work and his behaviour without making it too obvious to him. Because I've got to feel like assured.

Clearly Pat feels vulnerable and this means she is more open to persuasion by professionals and less able to be critical. Unfortunately, as she and Tony say, no professional support is forthcoming:

Tony: we're going into secondary education next year and there is no one you can go and see and say 'right this is what we want'. Everyone is sat on the fringes of it, you make the first move .. we've then got to battle to get the support of the teachers. No one will say. They all say 'well this is what you have to do', but there's no one. We don't want people to do things for us.
Pat: You have to do a lot of it yourself really. And we've got to go through all this but we've got to consider Christopher's needs as well. It's no use at the end of the day saying well 'yeah we're going to send him there' if Christopher is not happy going there. Because he's not going to come on if he's not happy anyway. So you've got to compromise then, haven't you?

The enormity of the decision to select a particular secondary school, is undeniable, and as Pat and Tony convey, the child's needs have to be paramount. The repercussions of an unsatisfactory choice can be extremely problematic as Maureen and Graham found out. When they were unable to get a satisfactory response to the episodes of Ian being bullied, Maureen and Graham considered changing school. Their description of support received, illustrates once more, how the experience of disablement is produced through unsatisfactory professional practice:

Maureen: there was Sea Grove, which we thought would be a good school but we had this chap around and he said he had to go to Higham school, to talk it over with them and what have you, and he said he would ring us in a couple of days, didn't he? And he never did. No, he never did. So I rang him and he said 'well, I'm not going to help you get Ian into this school'.
Graham: no, he said 'I'm not going to recommend that he be moved'.
Maureen: yeah.
Graham: you see without his recommendation, well, I mean you're talking to a wall aren't you?
Maureen: and audiology said 'we can't support him' and
Graham: no, they didn't actually say that,
Maureen: well, no they didn't,
Graham: they said if he goes to another school, 'we may not be able to give him the support that he usually gets now'. Which is exactly the same as what Maureen's just said [laughter]
Maureen: so, it was blackmail really, I mean we were put in a position, we

were on our own then. All the officials were against it, but we could see that the problem that Ian was having with the bullying, the school wouldn't deal with it. They were looking at it 'oh, he's a loner, he's one in the school'. But he is my son you know, and I thought 'oh, I've got no choice here'. But I did ring up to see if we could get transport, the school had accepted him, the Sea Grove school, but there was transport.

Graham: she would have to pay for it, that was the other thing as well, if you move on your own, at your request, you pay the transport. If the County says that he can go, the County pays for the transport ... well, what a smack in the mouth

Maureen: but you see because the audiology say, 'well, we don't think we will be able to support him'. Well, we haven't got any choice, have we? He needs that. Without that he'll just go forever back and back and back, and so that was it, and we just had to [stay put].

Maureen and Graham clearly identify how disability for Ian is socially constructed: 'the problem ... the school wouldn't deal with it'. Professionals, however, stick with individualised notions of disability and look for the problem within the child: 'oh, he's a loner'. As a teacher of deaf children acknowledges elsewhere, 'the sad thing is it is so easy to blame the kid' (Riseborough, 1993). Blaming Ian, though profoundly oppressive for him and his parents, is, of course, most enabling for service providers. In this case, they can resist changing Ian's school and the extra transport costs this might incur (we are reminded of Jenny: 'they want to keep their figures nice'), and they can exempt themselves from responsibility for developing and implementing a worthwhile anti-bullying initiative. Threats to entitlement are used to force Maureen and Graham to accept the decision of professionals, or as Maureen says: 'it was blackmail really'.

The events recounted by Maureen and Graham are so alarming, readers might wonder if there really was some misunderstanding or misrepresentation of what happened. But the tendency to remember selectively or to embellish the story is rigorously monitored throughout the dialogue; 'no, they didn't actually say that','well, no they didn't', 'they said..'. It may be tempting for professionals to dismiss Maureen and Graham's account as the confused haranguing of overwrought parents. After all, their son Ian's concerns were swept aside as if this were so. It would be easiest for professionals to locate the problem within the parents and we are familiar with the advantages of doing so. As we have seen before, if professionals consistently seek individualised explanations for a child's or family's problems, then they can abdicate responsibility for re-examination of their own role in the creation of difficulty.

Professionals oppress Ian and his parents by misusing their power over the provision of services. They do this in order to get their own way in relation to where Ian should go to school. This is oppressive enough, but what Maureen then goes on to speak of, reaffirms an idea aired earlier; if parents do not comply, then many professionals don't like it. What happens to Maureen and Graham subsequently, suggests professionals pulled out all the stops to make sure the family did not overstep the mark in future:

> **Graham**: when we fell out, where it had been all friendly and warm, it all went ice cold and the relationships went ice cold.
>
> **Maureen**: if you get your letters now, you get these official forms 'Dear Mrs Arden and Mr Wright' whereas before you'd get the same with 'Maureen and Graham' on it. You know it's all very formal now, and all we feel that we did was fight our ground, you know? They made us feel ... made us feel rough about that really.

In addition, we find fears Pat alluded to earlier come to pass. The power of parents to complain is indeed restricted because professionals can always vent their disapproval on the child. Precisely this happens to Ian:

> **Graham**: they used to have what they call a home to school book what Maureen could write notes in about Ian to his teacher .. and it's stopped
>
> **Maureen**: when we fell out they ended it.

But it is not possible, of course, in spite of deteriorating relations, for Maureen and Graham to retire gracefully and quietly agree with whatever professionals subsequently decide should be provided for, or conversely withdrawn from Ian. Shortly after the friction we have just reviewed, another problem comes along:

> **Graham**: they did this full report, the following April. The statement gets signed by Maureen, and they sign you see even if it's a bad report because then they've got to do something about it, because on a statement it says 'we have to give you all this help'. He has an annual review with the audiology [and someone] from the school and they started off by saying 'he's doing very well, he's 18 months behind and catching up slowly'. Now that's funny because they said that the year before and the year before ..
>
> **Maureen**: yeah but the year before, they said he was 12 months [behind]
>
> **Graham**: the year before he was12 months [behind] and catching up slowly, then two years later, he's 18 months behind and catching up slowly. Sense? *And* they're going to cut his time down with the teacher of the deaf, *and* they're going to cut his time down for in-class teaching with his ancillary, and the teacher of the deaf in the classroom, they are, that's what they said.

Maureen and Graham are in a cleft stick. Whatever they do will be seen as inappropriate. Either they allow Ian's extra support to be withdrawn even though the annual review suggests his development is falling behind, or, as they have done before, and as Pat and Tony did in equally contentious circumstances, they 'get stuck in' and demand better support. In the spirit most parents would take if they were asked to accept inferior educational provision for their child, Maureen and Graham do what it takes to ensure continued support for Ian:

> **Maureen**: there was a case conference going on
> **Graham**: the annual review, that's like the case conference, the annual review. Well, when he said that [support would be withdrawn] we hit the roof and there was big arguments
> **Maureen**: big arguments
> **Graham**: very big arguments
> **Maureen**: and really, it hasn't been the same since, has it?
> **Graham**: no... Oh we won, they give us more time
> **Maureen**: but in a way though
> **Graham**: we lost
> **Maureen**: we lost in one way because we weren't happy with the school.

Maureen and Graham realise their successes only partially alleviate a problem situation. If they are now disliked by professionals they have little recourse to alternative support.

We have quoted these problematic episodes at length because we feel they illustrate how the education and development of deaf children is determined far less by their hearing impairment, than by the attitude and actions of professionals who have responsibility for their support and enablement. Further conviction for this idea is to be found by looking at the successes and positive encounters parents were able to recall.

Positive partnership

When parents' views are respected and professionals endeavour to translate their wishes into practice, then deaf children and their families are enabled rather than disabled. A mutually beneficial dialogue can be established if professionals are seen to be genuinely committed to working collaboratively with parents. Jenny acknowledges this in her observations of how willing nursery staff were not only to listen to, but also follow up, her own ideas about Chloe:

> **Jenny**: the school that Chloe used to go to, prior to going to a deaf school, was the nursery unit at the school where my other children went and they were absolutely fantastic with her. Chloe got an immediate place and they went out of their way to try and find out everything to do with deafness you know, and wanted to learn sign, and [had] the enthusiasm to learn sign.

As we saw by looking back at Jenny's diary, Chloe's education was not problematic prior to the point at which professionals failed to recognise her parents' expertise, preference and rights. When Gillian finds professionals 'on our wavelength', Siân's education proceeds without undue difficulty even though she attends a school where teaching is in Welsh yet Siân's family language is English. For Siân to contend with two spoken languages, in an integrated setting at the age of four, not having had hearing aids until she was three-and-a-half, would seem a very tall order indeed. But we see with back up from professionals who regard prospective difficulties as their problem and not a child's, Siân makes pleasing progress:

> **Gillian**: there was a class teacher who was very sympathetic. The teacher, Mrs Powess, was wonderful. The peripatetic teacher of the deaf was very sympathetic, she seemed to be on our wavelength, I mean she'd got similar sorts of attitudes .. and Siân came on in leaps and bounds just by being with other children. They were very willing to do anything. It was a great school really in that respect. When she went to school they were supposed to teach them Welsh as a first language and Siân was allowed to have special dispensation because she was English first language and they needed to get some sort of language before she went on, so she's always had Welsh around her, but the class teacher used to make a specific point of translating everything into English for Siân. I'm not sure whether they would do that in every school. But because Siân was there they made a point of doing everything bilingually in a very structured way.

Helen, side-stepping for a moment into her professional role as a teacher, pointed out that efforts made to facilitate a deaf child's interaction in the classroom are mutually beneficial. With her 'parent hat' on, Helen knows how important it is for professionals to look beyond the child for the source of problems. Speaking in her role as secondary school teacher she comments:

> **Helen**: we've got a [deaf] child apparently in the primary school who's coming up to the secondary school in two or three years. And all the teachers in the primary school are learning sign because it's her only communication .. they have to understand what she's saying so they're learning to actually sign.

The child Helen refers to uses sign. If her secondary school teachers do not recognise her language, then her education will be characterised by disablement; compounding difficulties not only for the child, but for teachers too. To minimise prospective problems, staff are 'learning sign' to start ensuring neither they, nor their deaf pupil are disadvantaged.

There may be many new skills and strategies which it will be incumbent upon professionals to acquire the first time a deaf child is included in their school or class. But specialist training was not uppermost in the minds of parents as a pre-requisite for successful education. Being seen to make the effort to take parents' concerns seriously is by far the most important asset:

> **Gillian**: fair play to the head, he's very sympathetic and he's been very, very nice to Siân. I mean, most people will be a bit put off by having a child like that deposited on them two weeks before the beginning of term ... but fair play to him, he's taken it on board and he's been very sympathetic. He's been willing whatever I've gone in and suggested or asked him about.

This headteacher is managing to enable Siân in an integrated bilingual situation, and ensure her parents do not feel disempowered if and when problems arise. This shows professionals can take disablement out of the experience of hearing impairment for deaf children and their families if they have a mind to do so.

Similarly, the education of deaf children is less disabling if parents can exert their own wishes and have real choice in the selection of schools. Gillian can point to tangible ways in which both she and Siân would be disabled if their choice of school was overruled:

> **Gillian**: the biggest advantage we can see for Siân is the size of the school ... they've got 61 pupils and three teachers. We've got a brilliant ratio where they are now ... it's a very friendly little school, it's got a lot of positive things, everybody knows there is a deaf child somewhere in the school. In [schools with] 3000 kids some children aren't very pleasant. There are always some drawing attention to other pupils' disadvantages. The world is very selfish and I don't see that Siân would be as confident as she is if we'd been in an area where she was in a much bigger school. We're very lucky. The thought of Siân being swamped in an enormous secondary comprehensive fills me with absolute horror.

It is easy to see how, if Gillian's choice of school had been disallowed in the heavy handed way Maureen and Graham encountered, then education may well have become the deeply disabling experience for Siân and her family which it was turning out to be for Ian and his.

Who chooses?

Issues in choice of schools and control over decision-making are further complicated in relation to the question of how children themselves become involved. Although for many families this doesn't really crop up until choice of secondary schools comes on to the agenda, many parents were aware that their child's perspective might be different from theirs.

So Jenny, for example, who dearly wished Chloe would go to her local mainstream school accepted at some time in the future this might not be Chloe's own choice:

> **Jenny**: we've always said if she came home when she is this age [ten] and she wanted to go [to a segregated residential school] then that's her choice.

Giving children choices is complicated for parents in the same way as giving parents choices is complicated for professionals. Some difficulties may arise in putting it into practice because of the inherent power relation. The broad-mindedness that giving a child the choice expresses is curtailed if their parents genuinely feel they know better in exactly the same way as the liberalism professionals claim in giving parents choices is cut short when professionals think they know best. We cannot deny the power relation exists but potential for its misuse can be greatly reduced if it is openly acknowledged. Pat and Tony don't disguise either their preference or their control, but they are certain Christopher will not be denied their support if he chooses differently from them:

> **Pat**: it's interesting to hear what Christopher says really, because tomorrow evening we're going to, there's an open evening at Cherry Hill High school where he would go from where he is now but that's the only school he hasn't been to see so we said 'you've got to go and see it', but we don't want him to go there really, but I mean he's got to make his mind up.
> **Tony**: we've got ideas and he's come up with his own.

It emerges that Christopher is keen to go to a school which his parents are less keen on:

> **Tony**: he does actually feel as though he wants to go there ... it's going to be hard for us ... but he's got to go. He can get across that road there and get on the bus with all those lads. It's going to be hard for him at first but ... you know he's got to .. I mean he's eleven in February so he's got to start now gaining a bit of independence.

What we see is that unlike professionals, parents do not shy away from accepting and going along with decisions which respect another person's point of view over and above their own. Helen and Andrew allowed Katy a choice which they acknowledged had unsettling results for them:

> **Andrew**: we said 'you choose' and in the end you decided to become a boarder didn't you, to sleep there.

Whatever parents feel, or professionals want, or Deaf adults know, deaf children have their own role to play in making decisions about school. Parents acknowledge this and accept their children have to be listened to. Deaf children and their families would be greatly assisted if professionals would in turn, listen properly to them.

The politics of schooling

Just as individual professionals have power over families, however, it is true to say that in turn, yet other professionals have control over them. Sometimes when families find themselves being oppressed they discover those who deliver the oppression are being oppressed themselves. An exploration of the politics of schooling may seem unlikely to be an interest families would concern themselves with, but we discovered this is actually a key concern to many. This is because the political undercurrents which influence a child's education can be used by professionals as a mask behind which to hide a variety of shortcomings. Tony fathoms this out when he tries to find out why Christopher is frequently without specialist support:

> **Tony**: the teacher in the unit is also being used ... they were using her to teach music and things like that, but that's not what she's there for.

It is interesting to see again, parents do not tend to place blame within individual professionals. They are much more likely to see problems as socially constructed even though professionals rarely afford the same credit to them.

Maureen and Graham's account of the issues surrounding Ian's transition into further education shows just how transparent the politics of schooling are to parents, and also how they operate to disenable deaf children. Maureen and Graham are aware there can be a strong disincentive for service providers to maximise opportunities for deaf school leavers because of financial pressures in a climate of cut backs:

> **Maureen**: I suppose it comes down to money every time.
> **Graham**: what we say is 'Clive's got the purse strings now, he's got to watch his money'.

They know Ian is not restricted by hearing impairment, but by social situations:

> **Maureen**: he's going to be restricted when he leaves school because they don't cater so much for the deaf.

They suspect a great deal of thought and commitment will go into ensuring Ian is not a candidate for further education:

> **Graham**: they said he could go on to further education, but I don't believe them ... his education at the moment is beyond him and he is only twelve. ... I mean Ian's way behind ... he can't read. We don't know. I mean all the peo-

ple we do know, that we've battled with before, they'll say, you know '[he] can't do anything'. For the next two years everything will be hunky-dory, they'll say he is getting on fine, until he comes to the last annual review that we'll have just before his sixteenth birthday, then they'll turn round to us and say 'he's as thick as three short planks, he can't go anywhere'. That's what they'll do. Well, that's what they'll try to do. You can scream blue murder, but it won't get you anywhere if he's gone 16 and can't get the grades, he hasn't got the grades so he can't go to college, there you are.

Maureen: you see if he can't get them...

Graham: he's away then, he's not a school child any more.

They anticipate denial of opportunities will become more prolific once Ian passes the statutory school-leaving age:

Maureen: it's a hell of a struggle to get what we've got now, and now his schooling is compulsory.

Maureen can identify a simple and relatively cheap solution to enhancing Ian's prospects but doubts whether service providers prioritise her son's interests:

Maureen: they can put them back a year if they feel that it is necessary ... it's possible that they can do that, and we asked ... about if that would be possible for Ian and they say 'yeah, it's possible but we don't think that he needs it'. You know? So at the end of the day, if they say that to you, what can you do? If the officials say 'no, he doesn't need it' what do you do?

This is a brick wall they have been up against before:

Maureen: we were told that there is no way that Ian would ever pass the exam for [grammar school], so that would be a waste of time.

Graham: this was the officials that were helping us ...

What mechanisms enable parents to challenge decisions? 'If the officials say "no..." what do you do?'

Graham goes on to describe how professionals can easily use assessment as a strategy for deflating the family's expectations of Ian:

Graham: the argument now is 'he's reached his capability, he's not intelligent enough to get any further', this is what they're telling us now. But I always thought teachers were supposed to push the child because you don't know their limitations, just the same as you don't know anybody else's limitations ... This is why I said that when it comes to the last [review], when he's 16, they'll say 'he's thick, he hasn't got any grades for his O levels or whatever they are so you're out on your own Jack'. Which means 'there you are, he's your son, you get on with it now'. He's not their child, he's not in school, they've got rid of him. They've looked after him all the way through school –

they didn't do it very well, but they looked after him, they put up with him until he's 16 .. that's what they're going to do. That's what they think they're going to do. And I bet your bottom dollar they'll bloody do it and all. Because we don't know what to do. We haven't got a clue. Haven't got a clue.

The task of enabling Ian's access to further education falls completely on his parents. We feel it is wrong for professionals to burden families with this role because their endeavours can only be effective if they are backed up by those with appropriate resources and the necessary power. As Maureen says:

> **Maureen**: it just makes it so hard. Instead of families that have got disabled, instead of making it a little bit easier for them, helping them, *you seem to have double struggle, don't you*? I mean not only the child's disabilities you've got to cope with, but you've got the extra problems [of sorting things out] yourself (our emphasis).

Failure of professionals to engage adequately in ensuring education links to the preparation of deaf children for life beyond school, is tied up with low expectations of deaf children's achievements and a narrow view of what they might ultimately contribute to society. We would like to finish this chapter with some comments from Katy, however, which provide a strong case for imploring professionals to stop reproducing negative experiences of education for deaf children, and to take action instead to genuinely maximise opportunities for deaf children in their learning and development. Barriers can be dismantled in the education of deaf children, and what parents want for their deaf children, 'to be an ordinary person' (Tony), can be delivered:

> **Katy**: I went to university. I did loads of things .. university, that gave me a big choice. ... I want to set up my own business. I want to be a lecturer about deafness, about Deaf Awareness. ... I went on television ... I like doing lots of different things.

We return to the issue of deaf children's futures beyond school in Chapter 6.

Summary

What we hope to have shown in this chapter is that education matters for deaf children and their families are concerned far more with the attitudes and behaviour of service providers than barriers imposed by hearing impairment alone. Removing barriers to the inclusion of deaf children in an ordinary and successful school life does depend on adequate resources and political commitment, but many of the barriers could be swept away by individual awareness of disabling policies and practice. Dismantling barriers to education for deaf children requires professionals to examine the options they make available and to unearth prejudicial practices and attitudes which promote unequal access to opportunity and thereby disable deaf children in the classroom and beyond.

DISMANTLING BARRIERS

Families

Draw up a list of the three most important things which you want your child to gain from their education this year. Next to each item write down any things which might prevent your child from achieving the goal. Then think about what has to be done to break down those barriers. Make a list of people you will ask to help you. Write down the steps you will take towards ensuring your goals are realised. Look back at your notes in one month's time and note any changes you have been able to get off the ground. Have new things come to light which you could usefully tackle in this way?

For example:

something I want for my child this year –	her to join the GCSE French class
what might stop her? –	the French teacher doesn't think she's up to it
what shall I do? –	arrange to see the teacher to re-state our wishes; ask for a trial period
who can help? –	another family in a similar position; library might know of a French Club
review in one month	

Professionals

Make a list of any activities enjoyed by hearing children you work with, which deaf children are currently excluded from. Identify the barriers which lead to exclusion. Make a note of one or two strategies that you could use to start dismantling the barriers. Make a note of anyone who, or anything which, might stand in your way. Who can help you out?

For example:

non-inclusive activity –	singing in the school play
barriers which lead to exclusion –	deaf children lack confidence;

strategies for dismantling –

who/what makes dismantling
barriers difficult? –
who can help? –

other children teasing
discuss issues with class;
find out about sign language songs

little time to research possibilities
parents?
d/Deaf performers – perhaps
students from a local college or
Deaf Club?

CHAPTER 5

Shared Experience: Overcoming Barriers to Ordinary Family Life

Introduction

Stories presented so far show there is no such thing as an ordinary family. The conventional view of a nuclear family, consisting in two parents with a couple of perfect children is clearly a fiction as other writers have shown (e.g. Burman, 1994) and not just, in our study, because some children have impairments. Amongst the small handful of families who took part in this study, there are parents coping alone and parents embarked on second relationships as well as those in long and happy first marriages. There are appreciable differences in social class and economic background. The number of children in the families ranges from one to twelve. There are immense differences in life experience, living circumstances, values, hopes and expectations, many of which have by now become obvious. Having a deaf child may be the sole thing the families taking part in this study have in common. One mother understands her family's relative uniqueness from more than twenty years of experience:

> **Helen**: we've never actually met another family with a deaf child who we have anything really in common with.

We restate this point to emphasise that every family with a deaf child is different. Each family is taken up in a life of their own and if support is to be enabling then it must take account of this.

In this chapter our aim is to convey that there is more to family life with deaf children than problems in the management of hearing impairment. We look at strategies families have evolved for overcoming barriers which threaten their involvement with all kinds of mainstream activities and facilities. We talk here about joining the Cub Scouts, horse riding, trick or treat and teenage rebellions amongst other things, because participants have told us this is the stuff of which family life with deaf children is made. Deaf children and their families find themselves disabled, however, and oppressed, if other people's attitudes and environmental barriers restrict their involvement in the things they might ordinarily like to do. The way in which society responds to a child's hearing impairment has far-reaching implications for family life.

We highlight those issues which emerged as of main concern to deaf children and their families themselves. We continue to use the conceptual framework developed earlier to provide a way of looking at how disability can be taken out of the experience of deaf children and their families.

Knowing who can help

Looking back, parents had often found that in the early days following diagnosis of hearing impairment, lack of professional support led to the creation of barriers which prevented them and their child doing ordinary things. All the parents described the difficulty of having to seek out basic assistance where service providers are not proactive:

> **Maureen**: if you don't know what you are supposed to have .. how do you get it? ... [your] deaf child needs help, and you do. No good thinking that you can bat along without it. You do need to seek help and find it [but] as I say, if you don't know where to get it, how do you get it?

Families may be unsure where to turn when their questions do not fall neatly within the brief of any particular professional, for example in encouraging a child's independence. How to enable a child to go out to play alone, was a common worry and potentially detrimental not just for the deaf child, but for the whole family:

> **Jenny**: when I found out that Chloe was deaf there was no way she was getting over the gate, [her sisters] all had to stay with her, and I had to take hold of myself and say 'look, you can't restrict them because of Chloe'. I wasn't being fair to my other girls.

Jenny troubled further over this problem in her diary:

> 26th June
> The only thing I feel is unfortunate are my other two daughters, they have little or no time to play with Chloe, they would rather ride up and down on their bikes outside the garden, I do sometimes insist they play with Chloe, but am I right in doing so? I've always thought if you're forced to do something you resent it, I would rather it be a spontaneous reaction, so I tend not to stress upon the point too much, however, Chloe's content to have her dog or Mum around.

An important source of strength comes from families being able to address such concerns openly and honestly, but this requires non-judgemental support from others. There is no indication in Jenny's diary of any professional with whom she could air her worries. There is danger of entering into a cycle of oppression because the fewer chances deaf children have to develop their independence then the more dependent they will, in time, become. This can be seen from Jenny's comments. If Chloe cannot play beyond the garden gate then the outside world remains full of untried obstacles:

> **Jenny**: when she got to four or perhaps six she still wasn't getting out the back because she just didn't know about traffic.

Other parents battled with exactly the same dilemma:

> **Maureen**: he was older than a normal child to be going out [to play] you know, he was much older. But then I'd have to let him go, you know and he would go off and he would play, he'd just go off to the park, it's only round the corner, I'd give him instructions where to cross over, where to look, how many times and all this sort of thing you know, and he'd be tired of it really, you know what I mean, but that's how it was.

> **Pat**: the traffic was a nightmare ... if he ran on ahead I couldn't shout him. Just the simple things that you never actually consider, the things that you take for granted.

Since most deaf children are born to hearing parents, these 'simple things' as Pat describes them, could very usefully be the focus of family support. It seems deaf children and their families would greatly benefit if professionals could step outside of their role as the purveyors of high-minded philosophies and attend to some of these 'things that you take for granted'. A child's development as a communicator is after all closely tied to their developing confidence, and the latter comes with being able to play where other children do and having access to a wider range of conversational partners than a hard-pressed mum and the family dog. A familiar alarm bell rings again, however: once more it may not be in the best interests of professionals to agree these 'little' things make so much difference, because once again, it is probably d/Deaf adults, and other parents with deaf children, who are best placed to provide advice and guidance based on their first-hand experience of the reality entailed.

Voluntary agencies

Voluntary agencies, often run by d/Deaf people and sometimes parents, aim to provide help, support and advice to families with deaf children and can sometimes fill gaps in statutory service provision. Such organisations are, however, dependent upon charitable funding, and even though they step in where they can, themselves recognise a great deal of unmet need. Families contact voluntary agencies on diverse issues and express varying levels of satisfaction. In some of the letters received from parents, for example, we read of contrasting experiences:

> **Anne** (trying to come to terms with news that her seven-year-old hearing daughter could become progressively deaf): frantic with worry, I telephoned the National Deaf Children's Society who were so helpful. They couldn't talk about Amy's individual problem but they were so supportive.

> **Paula** (seeking general reassurance): we have joined the National Deaf Children's Society but I'm sorry to say we hear very little from them. In fact we have had no contact with them even after many phone calls and letters.

A parent we interviewed explained voluntary agencies can be inaccessible in a number of ways:

> **Graham** (needing advice on social security benefits): we've never been to a [local] Deaf Children's Society meeting because they hold the bloody things 60 miles away ... we tried the National Deaf Children's Society ... they just sent a very nice letter saying they couldn't help. We did have help from what's her name .. from the Deaf Children's Society ... but you see, [she] as far as I know, is one person and she had hundreds and hundreds of cases, but she helped us on the phone.

Joining in

In the absence of adequate professional family support, together with limited input from voluntary agencies, deaf children and their families find they have to struggle to do the things other children and their families do. But difficulties in taking a full part in mainstream activities are not caused by a child's hearing impairment. They are created because other people exclude them, or because access is denied or because other people are insensitive or unhelpful. Ian's experience of joining the Cubs illustrates this:

> **Maureen**: I could worry myself silly .. every little phase he goes through is a massive great headache. I mean the first time he went to Cubs
> **Graham**: yeah, oh my God, even with Cubs, I mean we still had problems with them ... it was as if Ian was just .. I don't know, part of the furniture I suppose, and they wanted to take him on because he was deaf
> **Maureen**: it would look good
> **Graham**: yeah, it would look good, 'we'll have him, he is a deaf lad', but that was it, he never did anything
> **Maureen**: you see Ian's the sort of chap, that he'll go somewhere, and he's not a trouble maker, he would sit there looking around, and he would be quiet all night. He won't get up and say, 'oh can I do this?' .. probably he knows

he's different, so he'll just sit down.

Ian's participation in Cubs is hampered by all of the disabling barriers identified above: exclusion, denial of access and unthinking others. Simply allowing hearing-impaired children to attend Cubs, or any similar association, does not, of course, guarantee inclusion, without which, deaf children are left out and isolated. The child's experience is disabling for them, and so too for the rest of the family:

> **Maureen**: I'm feeling terrible at the time, thinking what he is going through, but I know he's got to do it ... that night he went to Cubs .. I was looking at my watch every five minutes until he come up that road again. I couldn't wait till he come home.

On the other hand, when deaf children are not excluded, and efforts are made to ensure they have access to what's going on and other people show some sensitivity to their hearing impairment there is absolutely no reason why they and their families cannot enjoy exactly the same kinds of mainstream activities as anyone else. For instance, there are barriers to overcome for Siân and her family to enjoy horse riding, but they can be dismantled. Firstly there must be easy and effective communication:

> **Gillian**: Siân has to wear her hearing aid, she very rarely wears it for anything else, but she was aware that it makes a big difference for these riding lessons ... she watches far more and gets the feeling of what's going on by watching others rather than actually hearing, she gets the information but it's not as easy to get everything.

And secondly Siân has to have confidence for joining in. Her mum knows this is closely allied to being able to communicate. Inclusion, confidence and communication are the ingredients for enjoyable family experiences as the anecdote below shows:

> **Gillian**: she made me laugh the other day ... there were two girls who came in on our lesson three or four Sundays ago now, they would have been 13 or 14 ... the older girl had been given a bigger, more responsive horse and this started to play up ... she was having terrible difficulty making this horse do what she wanted it to do, and in the end it ran away with her, she couldn't get it out of the corner, it decided it was going straight in the corner and it would not come out. So my Siân quite off her own back, said 'I will sort it out' and she stomped across and she got this child off the horse ... [and said] 'get off, I will sort it out'. She got on this horse, well I had never seen anything like it in my life, she knocked this horse into submission [laughs] 'come on, get round' and she's giving it what for, she really did give this horse what for .. 'you will jolly well do what I say' ... once she knows, she can do it ... this horse behaved itself nicely for the rest of the lesson .. I suppose the main thing is

that she had enough confidence in herself that she could do it. She spent an awful long time building up that and it takes her a long time to be confident enough of something like that, but once you've got it ... she could say 'blow this, we're not having this, disrupting everybody else's lesson' ... she just took charge [laughs].

Similarly, Rachel faces obstacles when she goes to swimming classes but explains these can be overcome:

> **Rachel**: at swimming [playing team games] I'm not quite used to it yet because I never know if it's my turn or not .. but always at swimming I usually have Debbie .. it's always me and Debbie at the back
> **Eleanor**: can you understand what Mrs Morris is saying when you're swimming?
> **Rachel**: no, not really. That's why I like it when me and Debbie are at the back because when I'm at the front I don't have a clue what's happening
> **Eleanor**: but if you're near the back you can watch the others
> **Rachel**: if they're doing it right
> **Eleanor**: that's right. You have to make sure you copy one that's doing it right and don't copy one that's doing it wrong
> **Rachel**: that's why I like doing it with Debbie
> **Eleanor**: it's a complicated business!

It is important to retract the view of deaf children and their families as pitiful and absorbed with heavy battles to come to terms with hearing impairment. Siân and Rachel's stories remind us that deaf children and their families share the same interests and experiences as others. They may have to counteract prejudice, however, to ensure they are fully included, and this is a topic we will return to in the next chapter.

Access to information

Barriers encountered by deaf children and their families can be removed with sufficient awareness. Service providers often fail to recognise that disability is produced if they do not take account of this fact. Not surprisingly perhaps, in view of problematic practices presented already in this book, we uncovered considerable scepticism about how to enlist the support of professionals:

> **Graham**: keep making a pest of yourself. That's the only way you'll get anything, make a pest of yourself because they won't volunteer the information, they won't. Nobody volunteers. I don't care who it is, if they are professionals nowadays all they think about is money. 'How much is this going to cost us?' I would pester them and pester them and if they said 'you can't have it', I wouldn't believe them.

Graham's animosity runs deep because all sorts of barriers to Ian's inclusion in ordinary family life were shored up by professionals. Amiable television viewing, for example, was prevented because service providers prop up barriers to information:

> **Maureen**: we did find out from social services but this was way too late, that you can get things on loan. Now we got that amp there and when you switch that on Ian can hear direct through his hearing aid. He puts it on to 'T' then he can hear the television straight through his hearing aid .. but I mean these are the sorts of things that you don't hear about.

Jenny also encounters difficulty finding things out:

> **Jenny**: it is amazing how some people get to know ... I thought 'well how the hell have they got their information when it wasn't available to us?' ... they've heard of all sorts of things, like computers for deaf children ... and the lady from the deaf club ... she said 'have you not got one of those video-recorders that have got subtitles on them?' And I said 'I've never heard of them'. She said 'oh yes, you can get them you know, and you can get this that and the other'.

Most deaf children find watching mainstream television tricky as Siân explains, and as her mum reinforces, this can be problematic for the whole family:

> **Siân**: when I'm watching telly ... I can't hear *anything* ... erm people when they are talking, if they are looking somewhere else and I don't know what they are saying if they are not looking at me, I can't see what their mouth's saying.

> **Gillian**: she finds TV totally frustrating and so do I, because she spends half the time asking me 'what's happening now?' ... If we all sit down and watch it you have to spend half your time explaining because the plots are very convoluted. 'Why are they doing that?' and it's something very minor that they've told you previously but Siân hasn't picked that up and it's very, very subtle. [Her brothers] are fine and always saying 'explain that bit to Siân' ... to be fair to them, the boys are better at it than I am, they will just say, 'oh they said such and such' and go back.

There are barriers to information operating at several levels to disable deaf children and their families. There are obstructions when professionals withhold information about environmental aids and adaptations, and there are obstacles when television programme makers fail to provide access through BSL interpreters and/or subtitles. A recent major survey confirms 'deaf children want to be able to watch television for fun and information just like their hearing families and friends' (NDCS, 1994). Television plays a substantial role in widening children's education as captured in a note from Jenny's diary and a comment from Pat:

> 25th August [from Jenny's diary]
> Tonight watching telly, a robot came on and she was fascinated, she kept pointing at it and jumping up and down on her chair with excitement.
>
> **Pat**: it sounds silly, but even a programme like *Neighbours* is marvellous ... he's coming down stairs and he's saying 'such-a-body on *Neighbours*', a situation, you know .. and I thought 'well, what a load of rubbish *Neighbours* is' really, but actually he's learning things from it.

Everyday learning experiences in the context of family activities are quite needlessly 'totally frustrating' for deaf children and their families, however, if other people fail to identify and remove barriers.

Informal back-up

When families cannot get support from professionals, they turn, if they can, to their own relatives and friends. But sustenance is not automatically available from these sources as Pat explains:

> **Pat**: well, it's other people's attitudes, isn't it? [Friends] drifted away ... you know, when he was going through his bad patch, with his tantrums and his behaviour ... there's a few of those who drifted away and never came back really .. so that sort of makes you think about people's attitudes towards children that are classed as slightly different.

Jenny was able to talk to friends and family when 'nobody really' came to mind as having offered professional support. But as Gillian and Jenny point out, other lay people lack expertise:

> **Gillian**: our families have been very supportive but I don't think they could ever manage to see what it's like.
>
> **Jenny**: we've discussed it with family and friends. We're really lucky that we've got a close family and good friends ... I suppose we've had the support of family and friends and we have to work together and pull together and you get strength from that .. [But] like the questions people ask me, I feel stupid because I don't know the answers. Because they want to know, like we want to know, and you just feel stupid. It's my daughter after all, I just haven't got the information. It's not [that] I haven't asked, I have.

When families have to depend on friends and relations, they are quickly positioned as the authority on hearing impairment. When this happens, instead of being able to seek out reassurance and strategies for what to do next, parents can find themselves expected, though sometimes quite unable, to provide support for others:

Gillian: we knew she had a hearing loss, that was all we knew, and that she would probably have to have hearing aids. Nobody had explained to us how well or otherwise she would cope with hearing aids, how much good hearing she had, how much .. anything about deafness, it was a complete blank. And we had to go and explain to my mum and dad and Mike's mum and dad ... we couldn't explain anything ... so I'm afraid you just step back.

Friends and relations can and do provide enormous support for deaf children and their relatives. The trouble is that their back-up may not be enough and cannot be taken for granted; it is neither always assured nor unchanging. Increasingly, however, notions of 'care in the community' serve to exonerate policy makers from their responsibilities towards deaf children and their families. Friends and relations increasingly find themselves called upon to provide a range of support services from respite cover to paediatric habilitative audiology as the following quotes will show. The first two reveal the need for parents to have the option of alternative care arrangements, preferably from someone with appropriate skills and resources for looking after a deaf child:

Jenny: if I was in desperate need and I had to go somewhere urgently, I could quite confidently leave Chloe with anybody, whether they knew sign or not, and she would get by ... [but] it's trying to maintain that, because me and Doug aren't always going to be here for her.

Pat: [parents in-law] were marvellous ... but they're elderly and they're [living] up in the hills a bit really, aren't they? In the end [my mother in-law] started coming on a Friday and just let me go down to [town] ... she said 'right go out on your own, just walk round and have some fresh air and just not have constant mither or worry but just have peace of mind'. It did me the world of good. That Friday afternoon was just wonderful.

Gillian needed support for getting Siân to accept hearing aids – a task which often demands specialist tactics:

Gillian: [soon after being given hearing aids] we went to stay at Grandad's. Of course she thinks Grandad's wonderful ... and then she was putting [the hearing aids] in for a couple of hours or half an hour or something, but she wasn't having them in regularly, and Grandad said to her 'come on, I talk to you better and you will be able to hear better if you stick these in' and I think going there and seeing them be matter of fact about it and accepting it as normal, she took to it.

Relatives fill in for social services:

Maureen: if I had have had a social worker for the deaf that would have helped me a lot more. I don't know, maybe in a town, you might get more facilities and things. I suppose really my family helped me more than anything because I've got my family around, I mean if I didn't have anyone I would probably have coped less on my own, but you just got to get on with it.

Neighbours accept responsibility for extending speech and language therapy:

> **Jenny**: there is this little shop just at the end and I went into this shop and I thought 'well, I've got to start letting Chloe be more independent' so I went to the shop and said ... that I was new in the street and they knew that we'd got a deaf daughter .. and I said I wanted to start sending Chloe to the shop .. and they have absolutely been brilliant ... I don't want to send Chloe with notes, I want her to communicate with new people, because she's not always going to be with signing people, and sometimes she could be gone for half an hour and they will say to me 'don't worry about Chloe'.

Partners provide co-counselling:

> **Jenny**: if I sat down and honestly thought about what we've been through and what we've done, I'd have thought I'd never have been able to do that ... you wouldn't believe you would cope but you do cope. And you gain strength from one another. If I have trouble meeting a thing my husband is a prop and vice versa. You just do it, don't you?

It seems in these days of privatisation and cut backs to services, deaf children and their families increasingly 'just do it'. But is there any role in which the unpaid army of friends and relations are not obliged to stand in for professionals? It seems not. Maureen and Graham are even dependent on charity for the provision of amplification:

> **Maureen**: and then we got some money raised to get him better hearing aid, a radio hearing aid ... through the Lions Club.

And grandparents provide essential interpreting services:

> **Emma**: well actually [my] parents [are the most help] because you haven't got a clue what [professionals] are talking about when they come out with all this jargon ... I just can't understand them and I get really embarrassed you know, I don't know what [the audiologist is] saying and I don't understand what he's talking about ... I've got my mum and dad behind me ... there's me mother translating .. what he's talking about.

All of these roles friends and relations take on, however, show whilst there may be rhetoric for professional support of deaf children and their families, in reality back up is inadequate and bolstered by a great deal of good will.

Friends and relations are evidently invaluable. It seems there is no aspect of professional territory which friends or family somewhere, somehow will not move into if needed. This poses some interesting questions: why are so many ordinary people having to prop up professional service providers? And since this is happening, can professionals defend their role as the gatekeepers of resources? Friends and relations, it appears, are called upon not only to contribute to support of deaf children and their families, but also to exonerate service providers from their specific responsibilities for enablement.

We have already noted many of the responsibilities placed on these informal support workers need not exist in the first place. There is, for example, no necessity for professionals to use language which parents find oppressive. Even the most technical matters, describing cochlear implant, for example, can be dealt with in plain words:

> **Pat**: you could ask that man [ENT surgeon] anything really and he'd explain in quite simple terms, it wasn't beyond you, which I think is of great importance.

There is absolutely no need for the oppressive conversations which many parents are subjected to:

> **Jenny**: I don't know, people seem to talk to you in a different language, you know they don't use language that you'd understand, I mean they just fob you off ... they just sort of side track you all the time ... you know [they] just ramble on.

Aspects of practice which families consider praiseworthy show that relations between parents and professionals can be enabling, even if service providers themselves would acknowledge short-comings in service delivery:

> **Helen**: our peripatetic teacher was wonderful. Very, very supportive to us, especially me, because I was the one at home. She would spend the one hour with Katy .. she would then stay and talk to me for about half an hour. Support me through it, help me to know what was happening, show me what to do with Katy, you know ask me if I was feeling OK. Yes, and helped me to work through it. There was no-one else who understood.

> **Eleanor**: [the peripatetic teacher] was very nice actually, but we only used to see her about once a week and she had limited time. ... I'm sure if you talked to anyone else in our area [her] name would come up again and again. She was very good, very helpful really from the start until the time when Rachel went to school. ... But, of course, if [she] was away, if she was ill or having a meeting we didn't get anybody, nobody came, of course. Then there were the long six, seven week summer holidays when nobody came and it really, you know, you really felt that you'd been abandoned.

Shared experience

This brings us to the issue of families with deaf children providing support for families with deaf children themselves. Disillusioned with professionals, and sometimes others too, parents in our study felt the best source of support for deaf children and their families comes from people like themselves. They had found there were things professionals couldn't or wouldn't talk about but which families might tackle together. The main difference which seemed to characterise the view of support families felt they, as opposed to professionals, could provide, lay in acceptance that no-one ever knows best. Parents completely understood that their ability to put themselves in someone else's shoes was always limited and also, that empathy, often held in high regard by professionals, is only ever relative. This is an important point because it helps expose a key tension in relations between families with deaf children and the outside world:

> **Helen**: you can't just walk in and say 'I'm a parent of a deaf child and I understand what you're going through' ... I really don't know how you do it, it is very difficult. Because the doctor can tell the family that there is this, this, this, this and this and why don't you telephone, why don't you go along and see, why don't you go to a group, join a group or a club or something. But the family won't go you know, until they're ready. They need to be offered [support] more often, more times.
>
> **Andrew**: I think videos can be very good. Perhaps if you have the videos of the families and the families could say 'Hi, we're the Currys', you know, 'this is Katy and we can all tell you ...'. You [can't] say 'ah, just because that family and that family have a deaf child it means they will get on'. Not necessarily. It's partly luck, you know. I mean I think it's important to say that to families.

The reason Andrew felt videos would be helpful was because families could switch them off if they didn't like those providing the support. Or if they were feeling overwhelmed, they could postpone listening until they felt ready. No professional support we were told of was sufficiently flexible for parents to take up similar options, but the personal dimension of a relationship with a professional can be just as fraught:

> **Andrew**: it might be awkward ... you might spend an hour, you know, being nice to [someone] you didn't get on with.

The most enabling professionals were those with direct personal experience of deaf children and their families:

> **Jenny**: the teacher who came to visit the house, it was fortunate, she used to teach them at school and she was also the mother of a deaf daughter ... you really need that closer .. you know, people who have experienced it.

Professionals with relevant personal experience are, of course, few and far between but other families with deaf children are less so. Most importantly, families will probably have sufficient insight to make their offer of support flexible:

> **Gillian**: someone on hand, you know, just somebody you know, to say .. I don't know, I felt if we'd just had somebody there and had a cup of coffee to say 'well look, tell me your experiences', to see what they had, I know every child's going to be different, but as a rough guide ... I don't know, just that back-up, just 'you're not on your own, there are other people'.

> **Jenny**: when you are feeling low and depressed and everything's against you .. all these mountains you've got to climb you know .. just to have a talk or a chat you know and just it to be an informal sort of thing.

Several parents felt there was so much need for extra support they offered to provide it themselves:

> **Jenny**: I offered [to talk to other parents] after Chloe had been diagnosed deaf, and we had been used to her being deaf. We felt that if there had been another family who had gone through that who could talk to us ... and I've offered to do that .. you know, for newly diagnosed deaf children .. someone who will explain to you ... 'it's not as bad as all that eventually, after you get over the shock and everything'.

> **Helen**: I would like to be able to go into maybe hospitals and meet families who have a baby with problems or go and meet people with a six-month-old baby .. something like that. But I know certainly from myself and from other mothers they say, 'I'm not ready to actually receive that help. I want to be important and alone'... [some] mothers don't want you, they want to be left alone.

Notwithstanding Helen's final point, many parents with deaf children said they would welcome support from other families:

> **Maureen**: at the time there wasn't another family as such, that I knew, that had a deaf child ... it's nice to talk to somebody else and find out that maybe they've got a lot of problems more than what you have.

> **Eleanor**: yes, it's a great big help that. You think it's only you and then you find that somebody else is coming on a parallel pattern knocking on all the same doors and you think 'what a waste of time, we could all have done this together' or I could have told them 'I've done it this way' or she could have told me .. I think a lot of shared experience would be very useful.

The question of why ordinary families can't be the ones to assist other families, rather than professionals is raised. We were told, however, that professionals actually block opportunities for families with deaf children to take on this role:

> **Jenny**: we basically don't know who's been diagnosed as deaf ... it's just this withholding of information ... it seems to be a set thing.

The reader will guess that we interpret Jenny's experience as evidence that professionals have a vested interest in maintaining control and thereby reproducing vulnerability for deaf children and their families. The strength of interest amongst families with deaf children for supporting and enabling each other, however, is irrepressible:

> **Jenny**: we need reassuring ... it is normal to have doubts I would say, you've got to have the doubts in order to come through and look back on it ... but perhaps somebody else who is going through it can help.

> **Gillian**: I think that you need some sort of backup to be there if you want it. I'm not saying every family would feel the same way as we do ... some people want to venture out there alone ... somebody to fall back on, you know ... just ordinary people, parents who have been there and done it as a family not as a professional interviewing children or, you know, doing audiograms or whatever.

Families were not saying they did not want support from professionals. Rather, as the support they wanted was not forthcoming they had to seek alternatives:

> **Andrew**: we'd admit you do need expert advice you can't always get from a self-help group ... I think you need different kinds of help, different people... Looking back we didn't do very well.

In fact Andrew and Helen set up their own family support group:

> **Helen**: we started it with a whole lot of parents with handicapped children of all different kinds. And that was good, that was absolutely wonderful because then you met lots of families, you know, with different handicaps. That was good. It wasn't too precious or focused. So you could just support each other all the time.
> **Andrew**: it's not just support ... it [had] a target and it was a very active group, you know, used to campaigning and lobbying.

Other parents agreed their family support needs were not exclusively connected to managing hearing impairment:

> **Maureen**: I know it's not only problems with deaf kids because there is a girl .. she's got a boy who's autistic, you know, and she's had to fight all of her life as well, so it's not only deaf kids
> **Graham**: it's any disabled. Anybody. Any child who's disabled, any person who's disabled
> **Maureen**: you've got a deaf child or a disabled child so you will fight for the

rest of your life to get anything for them. That's what it's like, you will fight, you've got to. I think that's all the advice you can give really, just keep fighting because if you don't you won't get anything, and that child then suffers
Graham: why should other people go through it? Why the hell should anybody go through it? Why don't they just change the system? Too easy. Too easy.

Graham has hit on the heart of the matter. Disability has been individualised: 'you've got a deaf child'. The relationship between deaf children, their families and professionals is fundamentally unequal because families lack choices: 'you will fight, you've got to'. Other parents know this too:

> **Eleanor**: the only person who's going to fight for your child is you, nobody else.

Learning from families

Viewing disability as a social experience is something professionals may feel threatened by, especially if their practice is based on an individual way of looking at the experience of living with impairment. Service providers often do prioritise bringing about change within individuals. But as Graham says: 'why don't they just change the system?' 'Too easy' says Graham because the solution he has hit upon is obvious to anyone who actually does live with impairment. As we try to show in this book, the problems deaf children and their families face do not stem from hearing impairment; they are created by other people's oppressive attitudes and disabling environments.

There are obvious links back to mode of communication debates. Why does Lynas for example, insist 'the overriding concern ... is that deaf children be given every opportunity to make use of their residual hearing in order to understand and produce speech'? (Lynas, 1994). Why is there no regard for the possibility that 'the overriding concern' might be for everyone else to maximise ways in which they can communicate with deaf children? 'Why don't they just change the system?' Deaf children have enough on their plates without having to fit in with everyone else. What steps can everyone else take to fit in with them? If such an approach is not easy to implement, is this because too much power is at stake for professionals if they share their rarefied knowledge and expertise with d/Deaf people? Lynas is loathe even to concede expertise to parents:

> should it be parents, and parents alone, who have the final say in determining the education and communication approach offered to deaf children? Profes-

sionals who work with deaf children are committed to doing what they believe to be in the best interests of each individual deaf child. It is deaf children who are their clients, deaf children whom they are paid to serve, not parents. (Lynas, 1994)

Well, at least the cards are on the table. Parents, of course, will be asking themselves precisely whose children does Lynas think she is talking about? And exactly how does she feel the best interests of deaf children can be served without putting their parents at the forefront of decisions that will impact forever on the rest of all of their lives? None of these questions will be new to families who took part in this study. They were used to being given a back seat and being directed to believe professionals know best:

> **Eleanor**: the trouble is so many of these people think that they're right, you know, educationalists and medical people and so on, they just think that they're right, but just may be ... they have a limited information and they *don't* know your child like you do. In the end I think mums and dads have a gut feeling about whether it's going wrong or going right.

Emma intuitively feels some input from professionals is unacceptable:

> **Emma**: a lady that comes .. I think she's a waste of time when she's here ... because she sits and watches him, but to me ... [she] doesn't need to be there ... well, not unnecessary but a waste of time really. I might be wrong saying that, that's just how I feel.

Can it ever really be in the best interests of Emma's son for major decisions about his identity and future to be made by professionals whom his mother perceives to be so distanced from the real interests of this little deaf boy and his family?

It is quite predictable that Emma is unimpressed by the mysterious (unexplained) observation sessions. We have seen that she, like many other parents, has little reason to trust the judgement of professionals, unless of course, families will do exactly as professionals say:

> **Graham**: there is nobody to help, you don't know anyone. We don't know who to go to. Especially if you've had a fight with other professionals, then they're the last person you're going to go to and ask for advice. Especially if you think they've lied to you, or you think they're watching their pockets, or the county's pockets, which they are nowadays.

Well yes, they are. Another supposed truism from Lynas in her 'critique' of communication approaches for deaf children, is that bilingualism is 'a highly demanding of resources option' (1994). Baetens-Beardsmore, on the other hand, contests the commonly held view that integrated bilingual education is an expensive option citing several well-established and relatively widespread European models of bilingual education which 'fit into normal budgetary limitations with no or little extra cost attributable to their specific bilingual nature' (Baetens-Beardsmore, 1993). If professionals tell one version of this argument but not the other then families may well think 'they've lied to you'. When this happens, prospects for parents and professionals to work together are inevitably put at risk by those professionals who are paid to enable deaf children and their families.

It is not that easy for service providers to relinquish long-held power and set about changing themselves and their practice. This is where the challenge lies:

> **Jenny**: I think not only will families learn from professionals, the professionals have a lot to learn from families.

We couldn't agree more with Jenny. The stories we were told during the course of this project show, perhaps beyond anything else, that the lives of deaf children and their families are not one-dimensional. The nature of support they receive, however, very often is. Support is tightly focused on hearing impairment and fails to take account of other structural dimensions in deaf children's lives – like their pet dogs, or holidays, or brothers and sisters, and so on. We decided to use the last part of this chapter to make the gap explicit.

To start with, how sensible is Lynas's assertion that it is deaf children with whom professionals are concerned, not their parents? Parents themselves are aware of this rebuff, and of it's completely unrealistic ramifications:

> **Gillian**: I mean they tend to treat the child as the patient, but you are the poor unfortunate person that has got to deal with the hearing aid, when the dog chews it .. which is what happened [laughs] my sister's puppy chewed the hearing aid to absolute shreds just after she'd got it, and of course Siân was mortified, 'my hearing aid!' And you try dealing with a three year old who has got hysterical, got really attached to this hearing aid, and then find that the dog's chewed them and you're [on holiday and far from home].

Management of hearing aids is typical of the kind of thing on which professionals assume they are the experts, but parents think they actually know little about:

> **Gillian**: it's all the practicalities of actually dealing with it on a day-to-day basis, that a lot of the professionals just dismiss. And they do dismiss you. They do dismiss you as not knowing enough about it. And Siân's nine now, and I still have problems with some professionals who think that I shouldn't know anything about hearing aids and you've got to know something about

hearing aids if your kid wears the blessed things. ... Oh yes, you've got to make yourself blatantly anti-social sometimes. I mean, you are standing on their professional territory when you ask the audio technician in hospital if you could have a few extra tubes in case one comes out. You are standing on their professional toes and you have to be aware that you're standing on their professional toes. But at the end of the day, you've got to have some spare tube in the house in case. Because you can't be trekking of to the hospital at half past three on a Saturday afternoon and the kid is without a hearing aid. It's just not on. They do not realise the practicalities of dealing with it. It's just not reasonable or functional when going off on holiday on a Friday night and the hearing aid mould comes adrift or there's a crack in the tubing or the battery ... you've got to replace it then and there, you can't be hanging around waiting for it or going on holiday and spoiling everybody else's holiday for the sake of five minutes and being able to do it for yourself. And a lot of parents won't stand up to the sort of professionals who say 'this is my job and you can't have it'. I'm afraid you've got to. I mean, it sounds awful but you have to, you've got to do it, you have got to demand that they do things.

Gillian's reflection on 'professionals who say "this is my job and you can't have it" ' exposes precisely who many service providers are doing their job for. Professionals can add their names to those in power if they sufficiently mystify their tasks and responsibilities. If service providers disapprove of parents holding out for more information or access to their service 'you've got to make yourself blatantly anti-social'. Vulnerability is reproduced for deaf children and their families who find themselves needing to join forces to deal with some of these physical and social barriers which professionals impose on their lives:

Maureen: we've gone through .. like to the highest that we can, but you're just one person .. you know if everybody could fight, you know, *everybody* that's got these problems, if *everybody* had the time and the money to fight them then maybe, then maybe you might get some ground somewhere.

As Maureen realises, if deaf children and their families worked collectively this might reduce their feelings of isolation and strengthen their demands for real change. Perhaps this explains why Jenny, for one, has met service providers overtly operating in ways which conversely, reinforce isolation. Such a situation clearly demands further investigation if parental involvement can be taken seriously.

Another area in which professionals invest themselves with a great deal of expertise concerns parent guidance and counselling. A danger professionals often allude to is that families will become so involved with managing deafness they will lose sight of the child as a child (Luterman, 1987). A quick perusal of conventional academic books about children with hearing impairment, however (Bench, 1992; Webster and

114

Wood, 1989), shows very often it is the professionals who have lost sight of the child underneath, and if parents also fall into this trap, it may well be professionals who pushed them into it. The advice parents reported trying to follow, in Chapter 3, is prescriptive of problems Maureen comes up against:

> **Maureen**: when the second one came along .. I'm not being funny but I had a lot of problems with him and still do. ... He was only two or three and he would bite his nails and I used to get a bit worried about this and they said that because of the attention I've got to put on Ian, [Robert is] very jealous ... Maybe I did spend a lot of time with Ian and it was me all the time doing things with Ian ... whether Robert would have been the same if Ian were normal, you just don't know, you just can't tell.

Fortunately for professionals who influenced Maureen to 'spend a lot of time with Ian', she blames herself, rather than them, for problems created through having done as they suggested: 'maybe ... it was me'.

Getting on with it

Many parents felt that irrespective of explicit advice from professionals they had to prioritise the inclusion of their deaf child in their family over and above the management of hearing impairment:

> **Andrew** (to daughter Katy): it's important that we treat you like a child first and handicapped second ... it's important that the child does not become too much the centre of the family .. because the other kids suffer. Mummy and I were aware of this so for example you didn't like to go to bed. Eventually, Mummy and I said 'too bad, stuff you. You are the youngest, you are going to bed first so that Stephanie and Martin can have some time with us.' That's very important because if deaf children become too powerful and the whole family becomes obsessed I mean that's just .. bad.

Inclusion within the family is seen as the pathway to inclusion outside of the family:

> **Gillian**: we try very hard not to let her hearing problem become a major issue. It's not fair on the boys as well and it's not fair on the rest of the family. ... I have been to meetings where people have over compensated for their children and as a consequence their child, because it is deaf, thinks it can get away with blooming murder. ... And we've always felt that ... at the end of the day you let them go to live in a real world with real people and if they are anti-social nobody is going to want to know them.

We see that acceptance and inclusion of deaf children within society is much more important than insistence on sameness with regard to communication, as Jenny's diary illustrates:

3rd November

Today we went to Joshua's christening, the total thought of the occasion filled [me] with dread for the week leading up to today [but] was quite unnecessary. The girls behaved remarkably well and sang their own versions of hymns.

Afterwards we went to the Cock and Magpie pub for a buffet lunch. Chloe was yet again the centre of attraction. She really loved it. She was the one behind the bar dictating to 'Val' the landlady exactly what she wanted, and more to the point being understood. It was nice to sit back and look on as a bystander. Not once all afternoon did anybody come over to me and say 'what does she want? I can't understand her.' Although I can't say her vocabulary has increased any, but her ability to communicate is there.

Parents are much more concerned with acceptance of diversity than with making their deaf child speak like hearing children. Chloe's inclusion in the above scenario is facilitated because other people don't put barriers in her way. Jenny admits Chloe's vocabulary and communication skills are rudimentary. But more important factors for inclusion are in place. Chloe has the confidence to join in and this is encouraged because other people make the interface between her conversational efforts and their understanding *their problem*, not hers or her family's: 'not once all afternoon did anybody come over to me and say "what does she want? I can't understand her"'.

Celebration of diversity rather than insistence on sameness is what Pat too, tries to instil:

Pat: he came home yesterday and said 'I've been in music today', because he doesn't normally go in it you see. So I said 'have you been singing?' He tried to explain it to me ... 'well I was, whispering, sort of miming you know'. I said 'you can sing!' I said 'you know, it doesn't matter what noise you make you just have to follow' ... I said 'everybody's different, you can do it if you want to'.

Unlike many professionals, parents with deaf children do not necessarily view progress in vocal development as the most important thing. So what do they see as important? Exploratory play, developing confidence, shared experience and all the other things which are central in the development of any child as Jenny's diary shows:

1st June

We haven't been able to keep Chloe in the house these past few gorgeous days. She's enjoying the digging in the dirt, and the rolling on the grass and her main preoccupation is trying to escape through the garden gate. Another bolt has had to be fixed, as she soon mastered the art of lifting the latch.

2nd June

Chloe's first experience of a paddling pool. She copied the other children in stripping off and aids were eagerly pulled out of her ears. She enjoyed splashing and kicking in the water, a great day all round.

26th June
Chloe is still quite happy to play in the garden, her sense of adventure has got the better of her, she no longer confines herself to the path, but she now ventures on to the grass. This was an obstacle she has overcome, because the first time I placed her in the middle of the lawn she froze, she just didn't like the feel of the grass beneath her feet.

18th August [on holiday at the sea-side]
An absolutely fantastic time was had by all, we crammed everything in that we could in the space of a week. ... Chloe was astounded by all the goings on, the flashing lights in the amusement arcades, all the hustle bustle round the markets. At first I think she was confused by it all but she soon adjusted to her new surroundings. The beach was one of her highlights of the week, she loved this huge open area of beach and the freedom of being allowed to run up and down, through the sea puddles. She has no fear of new things whatsoever, and the excitement of all these new discoveries showed greatly on her face. ... Just to watch her was a great feeling for us.

The only cloud in this enriching summer for Chloe and her family comes from professionals:

18th October
We went to see Doctor Handley this week, and I'm afraid we were both greatly annoyed by the long waiting period, which we know happens, but the fact was when we got to see the doctor, we were asked three questions.

1. Can she feed herself?
2. Is she dry?
3. Can she speak yet?

I was very annoyed after one and a half hours wait to be asked three questions that on our previous visit we had been asked exactly the same. The doctor in question didn't seem to have a clue about Chloe, let alone to do with deafness. I'm afraid with treatment like this I doubt if they'll be seeing Chloe again.

Whatever support can Dr Handley claim to be providing? According to Webster (1994) counselling and guidance for families with deaf children is important for 'setting realistic expectations'. Well, Jenny's expectations certainly are realistically established. In the light of our research findings we suspect Webster is recycling a euphemism for ensuring deaf children and their families agree with service providers, who will find their job made easier if expectations are kept low. There is likely to be a continual source of abrasion here because families have high hopes for their deaf children, just as for their hearing children. One of Chloe's sisters wrote an example:

> **Joanna**: Chloe is really clever to say how deaf she is so I'm not bothered whether she is deaf or not, to me she's just a normal sister and I can't understand why people say that she won't know as much as other people.

The reason why service providers might 'say that she won't know as much as other people' is so that they can shift the blame if Chloe turns out not to know as much as other people, away from themselves. Any problem can be seen as Chloe's problem and not anybody else's. Even 12 year olds know this is unjust, however, as can be seen from further extracts of her sister's writing, and a friend's composition:

What it's like to have a deaf sister

Sometimes I find it hard to communicate with my sister Chloe, most of the time Chloe can have a full conversation without having to ask anyone what people are saying to her.

When we go shopping people are ignorant if Chloe is standing in front of someone's trolley and she doesn't realise people just bash her about and my parents and sisters and me all get angry.

On Halloween we plan to go trick or treating and everyone has said that at the end we should tell ghost stories in someone's house but they all forgot about Chloe and that she couldn't hear so I said 'if we have to do that then it's not fair and I'm not doing it if Chloe can't'.

by Joanna (aged 12)

What it is like to have a deaf friend

Sometimes I show-off doing sign language. Like doing the alphabet. Sometimes it is hard for me to communicate to Chloe. Sometimes she understands me from lip-reading. I enjoy sort of trying to communicate with Chloe. I try not to leave her out.

by Chantal (aged 12)

'I find it hard to communicate', 'people are ignorant', 'they all forgot ... she couldn't hear', 'I try not to leave her out': responsibility for easy and effective communication is not just Chloe's. Children can recognise and remove barriers. Why do professionals so often fail?

Growing up

As deaf children grow up and start to seek independence beyond their family, all kinds of new obstacles arise. They may come up against the full force of disabling barriers which others have placed in their way:

> **Jenny**: she's not meeting many new people as it is. She's got her sister's friends at the moment, who are really good but then I just hope that continues when they are older.

Tony and Pat talked about their efforts to ensure Christopher has access to the ordinary things teenagers get up to in which parents don't usually play a part:

> **Tony**: there's a lot of things, for the want of a better expression, that Christopher isn't very street wise about
> **Pat**: no, he's not street wise ... he doesn't hear what the lads are all talking about. He's coming home now which is nice, with bits of stories from the other boys you know just odd bits and pieces. Like he came home yesterday and I said 'did you thank Darren very much for inviting you to the disco on Friday? Did you tell him you couldn't go but thank him?' Well he went, 'well he's not at school'. I said 'oh dear is he poorly?' and he went 'ha ha! No'. He said 'Tom told me that Darren had picked the telephone up and said I'm not going to school because I'm poorly' and laughed ... He's started now to actually home in on these little conversations which is what he wants. This is not something I can teach him. This is something he's got to learn from the other boys. And he'll probably learn far more about life ... than I can ever teach him, you know. They teach him a bit of slang and things like that you know. But it's what's happening to the others boys as well, isn't it? Because we don't know what slang they're using, necessarily, not these days.

The importance of enablement as deaf children grow up is, of course, paramount both for them, and for their families:

> **Gillian**: the thought of her being a teenager fills me with absolute nightmares [laughs] I suppose it does for most people, the thought of teenagers generally, it's enough to frighten anybody but .. I mean she's got the added .. disadvantage, call it what you like, in that communication is a big part of teenage life.

There can be difficult issues for deaf adolescents and their families to contend with, but support services seem to be concentrated around the crisis point of diagnosis, and later on, families may find they have been left to struggle against the odds (Moore and Beazley, 1992).

In addition, deaf children also have to get through the usual barriers to acceptance which every other teenager ventures up against. There is probably nothing more enabling than a few arguments with parents, but these are denied to deaf children and their families if professionals have imposed limited communication skills upon the family. Most teenagers wrestle with their identity, for example, and for Katy such an episode was connected with her hearing impairment:

Helen: when Katy was about thirteen, she began to blame me

Katy: fourteen, I hated [Mum]. For about one year because I'm angry ... in a hearing world. ... I was saying 'I want to be hearing' for quite a long time ... and then for about one year, I hated her. She [was] very upset, crying. ... When I went to East Road school I learnt sign language. I find sign language easier, communication much easier. So then I forgave [Mum] afterwards.

Helen: what did we do about my unhappiness and your anger? We tried to talk, didn't we ? I tried to explain to you all the time. And I tried to love you as much as I could.

Andrew: sometimes I had to support Mummy and say to you 'no, it's not Mummy's fault' you know and sometimes I had to say to [Helen] 'it's not your fault'.

Katy and her family found this a difficult period. Only later, as we see in the next chapter, did they establish sufficient communication strategies to deal with these complicated emotional issues. Other deaf children and their families will be profoundly oppressed if and when these issues come up should the promises service providers made about language in earlier years have not come true. This is why, in the chapter on how to get communication going, we argued that professionals must operate with the very highest levels of integrity. And, as we feel the interviews brought home to us, hearing impairment is not necessarily the most important thing in the lives of deaf children and their families as Andrew confesses:

Andrew: we have some arguments sometimes ... I worry a bit that [Katy's] gone to live with Max [her boyfriend]. What happens if she can't get jobs ... sometimes I nag too much, but other times I think that for Katy's sake, you know, one has to fight for her ... it's very tight now. We all know clever children, young people with good degrees and they're not getting jobs.

And for Katy:

Katy: get the car [fixed] that's the only worry.

For Katy and her parents hearing impairment had not stood in the way of an ordinary life and positive relationships:

Katy: Mum, she's .. she's my best friend. And my dad too

Helen: it's a very good relationship. I am very lucky to have it.

Helen can offer some advice learned from experience:

Helen: know you're going to get through it. That's the most important bit of advice. Yes, it will finish. It's not going to stay there, you know, for ever. If you can actually talk and get through it, it finishes. [You] should be OK.

Katy and her parents are not simply 'lucky', however. They have worked hard to recognise and dismantle sources of oppression and disabling barriers. Ironically, the most disingenuous barriers deaf children and their families have to confront are those produced and sustained by professionals. We conclude this chapter with a story of disablement which we think helps to uncover what we mean.

A family wrote to us 'in case it's any use in your project'. They wanted their contribution kept anonymous because 'there have been frequent rows' and 'our son isn't around to give his permission'. In her written testimonial the mother told us:

I have learned a lot!

1. The sheer noise a deaf child can make.
2. The amount of work involved.
3. The up and down relationships with various officials.

The problems this parent cites are those which professionals are paid to enable families to manage. We feel that the third point exposes professionals as very often not attaining the goals of enablement which they are paid to pursue.

Summary

We have tried to show in this chapter, that the lives of deaf children and their families are not restricted by hearing impairment, but do involve an often up-hill struggle to break down barriers to their inclusion in a full range of activities of their choosing. The interviews reveal that it is both simplistic and inappropriate for service providers to generalise about the support deaf children and their families require.

Several suggestions have been made for how other people can offer support. Families see mutual support and self-help as offering great potential for dismantling barriers which they and their children face, and especially for helping to break down feelings of isolation and loneliness. The challenge is for professionals to overcome their own reservations about supporting self-empowerment activities, which might, of course, appear to militate against their own career interests. We feel there is substantial scope for deaf children, their families and professionals to work together to create enabling networks. For this to happen, however, it may be necessary to overcome disabling images of deaf children and their families, and this is the subject of the next chapter.

DISMANTLING BARRIERS

Families

Draw a picture of you and your deaf child doing something you would really like to be able to do in two years time. It doesn't have to be a very artistic picture, a match-stick drawing will do. On one side of the picture draw pictures or symbols, or write a few words to depict all the things that might stop you from being able to do what you want. On the other side, write or draw all the things you have to do to overcome the obstacles. It might be interesting for all the members of your family to have a go at this, and then to discuss together what steps you will take to ensure that you have the opportunities to do what you want to be able to do. Who can help you?

Professionals

Think about the kinds of activities you and your family enjoy. Do families with deaf children have the same access as yours to the things you like to do? Make a few notes on how thinking about the inclusion of deaf children and their families in mainstream activities and events influences the way you see your involvement with such families. What can you do to help break down barriers to an ordinary family life? Decide on some practical steps you could personally take to widen access. For example, if you have listed that your children enjoy gym club, can you write to the gym club in your capacity as both parent and professional to instigate ways of improving access for deaf children and their families? Can you support deaf children and their families in self-help activities? Who can help you?

CHAPTER 6
Images and Futures

Introduction

In this chapter we try to link images of deaf children and their families with prospects for their futures and to ascertain the role of others in promoting positive images and positive futures. We focus on image and identity, themes which to some extent have been reflected in previous chapters but which merit greater exploration as disabling stereotypes were often at the root of problems which families placed on the agenda in the interviews.

We want to raise awareness of disabling imagery in everyday life and to consider some implications of the images which are held about deaf children and their families. We also wish to reflect on how families contend with stereotyped portrayals and in doing so, to affirm the importance of positive images for deaf children and their families.

Many negative images threaten the well-being of deaf children and their families. Charities and voluntary agencies may have some responsibility here as the advertising campaigns often use images which position deaf children and their families as in need of patronage or pity to draw money from a benevolent public. Equally as disabling, though less pathetic, are images of deaf children and their families as immensely courageous and in need of a well-earned pat on the back. Many disabled people object to both of these sets of images (Barnes, 1992; Keith, 1994; Morris, 1991, 1993). This is because such portrayals equally misrepresent the lives of ordinary people with impairments; the former imply deaf children and their families are a burden, whereas the latter suggest impossible goals and that, in addition to living with impairment, deaf children and their families need to be super-human whilst they go about it.

The problem of stereotyping is, of course, compounded for deaf children and their families because they experience prejudice about impairment in addition to sex, race, age and other common types of discrimination which most people face in one form or other in our daily lives. This means deaf children and their families may be marginalised and discriminated against because of a wide range of prejudices and assumptions, and the likelihood that they will encounter prejudice and disabling barriers is considerable.

Disabling imagery has a direct bearing on the way deaf children and their families view themselves, and especially upon the way in which deaf children feel about their place in society. In this chapter we explore various images held about, and by, deaf children and their families. We consider the extent to which these images are oppressive and disabling. Lastly we consider the implications of imagery the families describe for empowerment of deaf children and their families.

Disabling pity

A frequently occurring public image of deaf children and their families is as in need of pity. The roots of this portrayal could be debated but the outcome is disabling to both children and their families. Pitiable images create a feeling that there is little that can change the family's lot, but the doling out of a generous dose of sympathy will at least make others feel better. The damaging implication is that the situation of deaf children and their families is hopeless and that neither deaf children themselves, nor their families can do anything constructive towards making their experience positive. Gillian found herself on the receiving end of such a view:

Gillian: Mike's parents do tend to do it a bit ... I don't think deliberately, and I'm not trying to criticise but it's just an observation that [they] tend to portray her as 'the poor handicapped child syndrome' and I find it very demeaning but a lot of people will do it.

This type of image has serious consequences. It may be hard for individual children assigned to such a role, to break out of the ascribed mould. Fortunately for Siân, her close family and its wider network of relatives and friends had a much broader view of her role in the community. Gillian recalls with pride and delight a real image of the confident, capable and independent member of the family which Siân actually is:

Gillian: she was a bridesmaid last year, one of these grandiose performances ... Siân thought it was absolutely wonderful. The day of the wedding, I dropped her off at ten o'clock, they were in the hotel, they were having their make up and their hair ... and Madam decides to have her own hair do. This was all her idea she will have her hair upwards so she had the hairdresser organised to do the hair do .. [laughs] .. so they came down in the car with the dress and then Madam is there with bundles of dress stuck in her arms 'you mustn't get this dirty Aunty Bethan' [laughs] .. she's giving her lectures, took her job very seriously held the bouquet and organised the page boys in the church and she really did, she got back to reception and she wasn't still from half past four in the afternoon till eleven o'clock when we had to practically drag her out ... and everybody said to me 'oh she's been round and talked to us' and she'd been round and talked to every single person at the wedding reception .. and everyone said 'isn't your Siân wonderful'.

Siân is absolutely not the 'poor handicapped child'. Hearing impairment does not stop her from leading a full life. When other people assume she is a 'poor handicapped child', however, or make other assumptions about her, then disabling barriers are put in her way. Gillian relates this to experiences at school:

> Gillian: the previous school had babied her a lot ... they had preconceptions.

Service providers may, however, find it useful to fasten on to images of deaf children as 'pitiable' because this allows them to distance themselves from responsibility for enablement. Positioning children as pitiable can, ironically, reduce expenditure:

> Jenny: [with] the money that was left [from closing Chloe's school], they took all the children to America for fifteen days which .. I think it was like a soft soap thing.

By exploiting the image of deaf children as pitiable, the Local Education Authority can position themselves as generous and kindly disposed towards deaf children, and this conveniently deflects from the fact that they had swept parental choice aside. Photographs of the chosen deaf children appeared in the local newspaper ensuring that the children actually assist in making professionals look good and bounteous. Deaf children were positioned in ways which recycled negative images and which in doing so, furthered their experience of disablement. The careers of the relevant LEA officers, however, are in contrast, presented in a most enabling light.

Enabling difference

Predictably, parents have misgivings about other people looking upon their deaf child as if of novelty value. Gillian recalls benefiting from a new health visitor soon after Siân's deafness had been diagnosed but feeling a little sceptical about the approach:

> Gillian: the new health visitor was brilliant, she was very very good. She came round, she sorted, she was completely different from the old one. Whether that was because they'd suddenly discovered they'd got something that was a bit different and a bit unusual, I mean they like to have something different, something unusual on their patch.

Whilst it is certain that Gillian was pleased with the way things had changed, this nagging thought about the underlying motive heightened her feelings that the family was now one that would be viewed as 'different' and interactions thereafter might all also be tinged with the novelty factor. Gillian might be prompted to wonder whether the service exists for Siân's benefit, or whether Siân's problems exist for the service. Families were familiar with this sort of response and its disabling consequences if they and their child were set apart from others.

In contrast to the rather calculating interest which parents felt adults sometimes exhibited towards them and their deaf child, when children are innocent perpetrators of curiosity parents link this with prospects for the development of personal identity, enablement and inclusion:

> Monday 3rd June [from Jenny's diary]
> I took Chloe on the bus to visit a friend, her little boy was quite besotted with Chloe's hearing aids. She allowed him to look at them but as soon as his hand reached out to touch them she went berserk. She now regards them as her personal belongings. A very good day, not as frustrated with her disability.

There is a great deal of personal significance for Chloe in the experience related above, because the event involves other people in coming to terms with her deafness and not just herself, alone. Emma sees the value of similar encounters for Sam:

> **Emma**: he gets children coming up and like looking at his ears. But the nice thing is they ask, you know ... they come up to me and ask what I'm putting in his ears and I explain that 'Sam isn't able to hear the same things as you and these help him hear the same things as you.' I try, and it might not be correct, but to me it's the easiest way to explain. They probably don't understand anyway but it's nice they ask. All right they stare and what have you and that bothered me at first but it doesn't any more.

Professionals have sometimes viewed such approaches from non-deaf children as making life more difficult for their deaf peers (Pound and Moore, 1989). Parents, on the other hand, saw prospects for personal and social development for both children:

> **Gillian**: she'll be about six or seven .. and we were in a shop somewhere and another smaller child came up to her and they were chatting away. Suddenly this child said to Siân 'what have you got those things in your ears for?' And without batting an eyelid or making a fuss or anything, she just said 'oh, it's because I can't hear very well and I have to wear these' and that was the end of it. She didn't make an issue out of it, she didn't sort of go into long detailed explanations, I don't think she worried or anything, and this other child just accepted it and carried on.

Eleanor did not feel uncomfortable about interest from other children, saying:

> **Eleanor**: usually it's just curiosity if anybody asks anything at school, it's not sort of malicious.

These excerpts typify the way deaf children and their hearing peers are prepared to accept hearing impairment as a non-problematic dimension of personal identity. Inclusion is an important determinant here, however, because we have seen before, segregation and exclusion has over the years bred ignorance and hostility.

Deaf but *not* dumb

Emma is aware of prejudice at large and, indeed, of her own in different circumstances:

> **Emma**: they are deaf but they are not dumb ... you still hear people saying 'deaf and dumb' and you kind of expect it but when you are confronted with a problem yourself, you know that child is not dumb. And you know it gets you really mad because people do say it. Even like relatives, older relatives you know, not actually said that Sam is deaf and dumb, but [they] meant somebody else is deaf and dumb.

Deaf children themselves, and their families of course, pick up this oppressive image which associates hearing impairment with learning difficulty. Several reflections were made on the pain that this creates. Siân, for example, aged nine, expressed anxieties over this very matter:

> **Gillian**: she knows she's not stupid and she'll say 'I'm not stupid just because I can't hear'. She will actually say that ... she says things to me like ... 'why do people think I'm stupid just because I'm deaf?' ... she's aware that ... people aren't being quite as she expected them to be, or people aren't being quite as sympathetic and she is aware that she has difficulty.

The disabling effects of such assumptions have been considered in the previous chapter, besides which, they are quite self-evident.

A particular aspect of the 'deaf and incapable' attitude towards hearing-impaired children, which troubled several families, was the resultant over-articulated, exaggerated speech people produced in the belief that it would aid communication. Maureen, Gillian and Emma all take exception to this:

> **Maureen**: you get many people ... who will look at him and say [mimics slow exaggerated speech] 'HELLO-IAN-HOW-ARE-YOU-TODAY?' .. I could wring their necks, he's so embarrassed. I used to .. say 'he's very well, thank you' because he felt so bad he couldn't speak so we just used to walk away. I

don't think enough people understand enough about deafness.

Emma: I don't want people going 'ARE-YOU-ALL-RIGHT-ROBIN?' you know, talk to him like that .. it gets me mad.

Gillian: people do talk *at* her rather than *to* her a lot of the time.

There is a great deal of anger about the assumption that children with impaired hearing have problems making sense of what is going on around them because deaf children and their families know this tenacious misconception is a hard one to break down. Jenny was very distressed thinking of the way society might treat Chloe, based upon her own observation of a deaf woman in a hospital ward:

Jenny: nobody could communicate with her, so they sent for me to speak to her ... to tell her that these tablets she had to take were painkillers .. and she was telling me that 'they said I'm stupid', because she could lip read you see, 'they said I'm stupid and I'm not stupid'. She was really angry and wouldn't even listen to me at first. I tried to touch her, you know, get her attention, she wouldn't look at me, if she won't look at you, you know she can't .. you're not there as far as she's concerned. I tried to tell her 'I've got a deaf daughter and it's all right, I can sign a little bit', etcetera, and that they weren't trying to harm her ... well, when I came home that night, it dawned on me that one day Chloe's going to be like that and is everybody going to think that she's stupid? This is what [sobs] .. I'm sorry .. I get .. it's all right .. is everybody going to think that she's stupid? Because that woman, although in a ward full of people, she was alone.

This is a very poignant account, not only of the suffering someone has had at the mercy of oppressive and unjustified images of deafness, but also of the dread that fills a parent as they take in the appalling outcomes of prejudice and disabling stereotypes.

Is science the way out?

It is easy to see why, when families come up against so many oppressive images in their everyday lives, they might wish their child could be hearing:

Jenny: perhaps some day there might be that miracle cure ... somebody's going to wave that magic wand. I know I'm living in fairy tale land, but you've got to have hope. You don't know, the way medicine is progressing now .. perhaps not in her life time. I don't know but in the future .. but I am happy, she is happy, she's a happy girl.
Gillian: [representatives from a national pro-oral agency] they kept going on about the developments in technology and all this ... I think Mike is more

[keen] than I am, he's very won over to that point of view, he thinks that science is the way out.

The trouble with the quest for a cure is that it may distract children and their families from acceptance of impairment (Oliver, 1993b). Beyond the family, the quest for the cure exonerates service providers from concentrating their efforts on enabling strategies. Thus 'miracle cures' may provide 'a way out' as Siân's dad calls it, but not for deaf children and their families; rather a way out for professionals who would sooner insist upon sameness than facilitate diversity.

Jenny says 'I am happy, she is happy, she's a happy girl', but a myriad of disabling barriers and experiences of prejudice and discrimination, continually threaten the identity of deaf children and their families. At least one mother found the image of deaf children as in need of a cure offensive and oppressive:

> **Eleanor**: one night [a friend] came to pray for Rachel and we were very grateful for the support, and she prayed that Rachel would be healed and I really thought this was wrong ... I felt 'this is Rachel, and if she's deaf she's still Rachel'. It's not 'she's not quite perfect and if we can't cure the deafness she never will be'.

Christopher's situation is very different. When we spoke to his parents, he was adjusting both to having lost his hearing through meningitis five years earlier and to the implantation of a cochlear device some twelve months prior to our meeting.

The sudden onset of hearing impairment following meningitis distinctly threatened Christopher's identity. Pat recounted some of the outward signs of the change:

> **Pat**: after having a child for four-and-a-half years who's such a good conversationalist and demanding conversation really, wanted to know how everything worked, very inquiring mind, always asking questions, enjoying discussing, even a normal trip to the shops he wanted to know how the sun worked, and how the moon worked and where does the wind come from. He wanted to know all these things and we'd have quite good conversations on the way to the shops and things like that. And he talked to everybody we met along the way. He could never be the same at that time. He wouldn't speak to anybody, he wouldn't let me speak. He wouldn't let me stop and talk, he kicked me and took it out really. He got so frustrated that he couldn't join in the conversations and that things weren't the same for him. And I got frustrated observing him and his behaviour had changed.

The family went through many painful experiences together after that time and eventually some four years later Christopher underwent a cochlear implant operation. Pat and Tony also tried to keep in mind that it

Was not a 'miracle cure' but the messages about this from professionals came across as mixed:

> **Pat**: I mean nobody could have worked harder not to build his hopes up too much than the [team] did ... but I can't help saying that they are waiting, they are hoping for a miracle.

Precisely what kind of miracle is hoped for? Deaf adults interpret cochlear implant surgery as an attempt at 'getting rid of deafness' and deplore the 'individual pathology' model to deafness which underpins the operation (Ladd, 1991). It is known that advocates of cochlear implants often exclude Deaf people from discussions on their service because of their implacable opposition to implantation of children (Lane, 1994). Accordingly, we would argue the desired miracle has less to offer deaf children and their families than to the professional team. Deaf adults know that children are not necessarily disabled by hearing impairment, but suffer oppression in a world of prejudice and disabling barriers. A much more attainable miracle might involve the dismantling of some of these barriers so that deaf children can be enabled by other people with whom they share their world, without dependence on a three to four hour operation to implant the latest piece of *experimental* technological wizardry.

Pat reports that the benefits of Christopher's surgery were varied:

> **Pat**: at first it was wonderful because .. he's so excited about it himself and obviously we are ... I mean I couldn't believe it really, I mean the first, when we'd been for switch-on day and we'd gone out at lunch time he went 'oh..' I said 'what's to do?' He said 'was it a lorry?' That's the first thing he said to us. When he went out he was looking round and I don't think it was a pleasant noise, but I think he was amazed that he'd heard something. I think he was frightened really.

The operation itself left its mark:

> **Pat**: the only thing that Christopher was upset about was, which I was surprised at really, was the scar. He cried, tears running down his face. We were in the bathroom and we took [the bandage] off and he did get a bit upset which I was amazed at, I would never have thought he would have done ... it was quite a shock to him.

Further, cochlear implant brings disabling obstacles of its own:

> **Pat**: you know like Christopher still gets times where, I think if his equipment was easier to wear I think it would be better. I mean he's so fed up with this bulk coming out and for a ten-year-old boy that's running about, the equipment is not ideal. I have to say that. But he puts up with that because he gets the benefit from it. But it is a nuisance to him. But having said that there are

times in his life that he wishes he could just hear like everybody else, still,

and may create barriers to inclusion:

> **Tony**: the only thing [the surgeon] said, as we were going in hospital, was about sport ... he said 'the one thing you must never do is play rugby', he said 'not unless your the fastest man on the field by a long, long way'
> **Pat**: that's a disappointment to him though, he loves to play
> **Tony**: he's always wanted to play rugby ... we can't really tell him 'no he can't' till .. we'll leave it. We were putting it off really but just trying to keep his spirits up with everything else.

One outcome of Christopher's operation was that he was able to hear the telephone:

> **Pat**: [he was] really excited and I was, he'd never heard the telephone for five years.

However, telephones are, of course, accessible to d/Deaf people without cochlear implants. When Katy was living away at university the family obtained a minicom:

> **Helen**: oh, the feeling that night [of the first minicom call] for me. I mean after years of her living away ... I cried and cried because we had a half-hour, *a half-hour* conversation ... I think it reiterates the point that people need help in different ways. You know they need lots of support and love and understanding but they also need simple things like good machines.
> **Andrew**: when [Katy was] 21, suddenly [she] could telephone her friends for the first time in [her] life. So that's the good side to technology.

The cochlear implant may have brought some rewards. However, Christopher still has the huge task of dealing with the drawn out impact on his identity. Christopher seemingly, did not see himself as a deaf person:

> **Pat**: there are times in his life that he wishes he could just hear like everybody else still ... there are still odd times where you know 'I want to hear, I don't want to be deaf' you know, I must admit he does say it ... I think he's hoping that they'll sort it all out and come up with a miracle and he'll get it back. I think he still hopes you know ... Like, he said to me this week .. he was watching something on the television about research into something. And he said 'why don't they find out about that bug that's gone in my ear?' ... I think he's hoping that they'll sort it all out and come up with a miracle and he'll get it back. I think he still hopes you know. I've said 'well it's damaged, your ears [are] damaged now but you've got your implant. You're very lucky, some people haven't got that', and we go on and on and on and try to explain to him that, erm without actually saying 'it's never going to be like it was' but he's been deaf longer than he's been hearing.

Whilst Pat has become quite proficient in signing over recent years and enjoys meeting people in the local Deaf community, Christopher:

Pat: absolutely hates anyone signing to him ... [he says] 'well don't do it to me, for Deaf people that, don't let anybody see you do that'.
Tony: that's his own opinion, nothing's been pushed down his throat.
Pat: if he wants to join [the Deaf Community] when he's older that's entirely up to him.

Lane (1994) asks what the purpose of cochlear implant is, given that deaf children have access to language and communication without it. Other obstacles in deaf children's lives, such as all those which present barriers to inclusion, are socially created and can be dismantled. Many commentators feel that the purpose of cochlear implants is to surround deaf children with problems that Deaf adult's can play no part in alleviating (Ladd, 1991; Lane, 1994; British Deaf Association, 1995). This brings us back to the notion that vulnerability can be created for deaf children and their families, through insistence on sameness which engineers the self-aggrandisement of hearing professionals.

Cochlear implants are typically viewed as offering possibilities for deaf people to become more like people who are not deaf. But we have mentioned before, on a number of occasions, how the desire for sameness that can permeate the lives of deaf children and their families can be oppressive. In our view, there is a deep-seated need to value and celebrate difference for genuine inclusion. Families recognise many barriers when other people fail to acknowledge difference and we will turn to this next.

Invisibility of deafness

A lack of outward indications of deafness can render deaf children vulnerable to being ignored:

Andrew: I think one thing you realised is that the public didn't realise that deafness was a big problem because they used to look at [Katy] and think 'Oh, she looks fine. She's a happy baby and she's making noises, she's running about.'

The invisibility of deafness can be disabling as there is no signal to others that the child and family may have different requirements. Katy, for example, continues to run into difficulties:

Andrew: it's the old invisible handicap. [To Katy] Remember when we got on the bus today ... I said 'we're going to the station' but you don't ask for the station do you?

Katy: No. [I ask for] Royal Parade. If I say 'station' he can't tell [where I mean].

Andrew: yes, it's like when you used to drink Coca-Cola.

Katy: I hate it.

Andrew: but the bar staff could understand ... she told me that a few years ago she would say other things and they would say 'what? eh?' and then [she] used to say 'all right Coca-Cola'.

Katy is keen not to stand out. Vulnerability is created by other people's reluctance to tackle her impairment. The more invisible she makes herself the more she is disadvantaged, but if she doesn't attempt to disguise her impairment she is treated as an oddity, and people draw unwelcome attention to her: '[people] say "what? eh?" '

A lack of visible impairment can create a conflict of desires when deaf children and their families wish to be easily and fully accepted, but also want to ensure that their needs are wholly recognised. Gillian felt an oppressive image of Siân as 'normal', stemmed from Siân's use of speech and not sign, and that the family were strongly disadvantaged by this as many problems went unrecognised:

> **Gillian**: because you are oral [people think] you are not deaf ... And these kids have got something wrong with them and they do need people to be aware of it, and if the people who are supposed to be sympathetic and the people who are Deaf dismiss these kids as oral, as being 'oh, they're normal' ... the message is going to come back from the Deaf Community that these children don't need any help. But they forget about their problems and all that. I mean the medical professional are very good at that, they dole out these hearing aids as if 'oh, like your hearing's normal, and it's like putting a pair of glasses on'. It isn't. It isn't like that. But it's very hidden the complications in life that there are.

The complications Gillian alludes to, when people lose sight of the fact that deaf children actually have impairment, can be very problematic. Such impressions (and their subsequent barriers) often stem from well-meaning, though clumsy, attempts at inclusion:

> **Gillian**: we spend a lot of time with my mum and dad, and my mum and dad are less conscious of her as a child who is deaf ... they are the other extreme, they just dismiss it totally and that's the end of it and you just have to start popping up every now and again and say 'well, she can't hear you, you can't expect to hear you when she's down the bottom of the garden and you've got an electric saw going twenty to the dozen, she just can't hear you'.

Barnes (1992) argues that regarding children with impairments as 'normal' is another form of oppression which serves to release policy makers from significant areas of responsibility for providing support:

> **Eleanor**: the teacher told me Rachel's not what they would call a special educational needs child because she is too bright .. although she has a special need .. but not what they count.

What have you got those things in your ears for?

Common misconceptions about hearing aids may perpetuate the deceptive idea that deaf children may not actually have impaired hearing. Several parents expressed frustration over this:

> **Gillian**: people have got to take into account that her hearing aids don't make her hearing perfect.

> **Eleanor**: if the moulds are cracked [Rachel] says 'it sounds like your talking to me through a puddle'.

> **Jenny**: people's assumption [is] that because she's got a hearing aid that she can hear normally, that is another thing. [They say] 'what do you mean she can't hear?' .. I always say, 'if you're under water you can hear noises and that's all them hearing aids are doing ... making the gargled noise sound louder'. And that's my explanation to people. They think [the hearing aid] clarifies and .. it doesn't clarify.

The need to explain constantly is wearing, especially as families have little control over how attitudes may be altered by their efforts to raise awareness:

> **Maureen**: people think 'he's deaf and he's got hearing aids so he's all right .. the hearing aids have corrected it'. And you explain it, you know, for so long, but it goes in one ear and out the other, so that in the end you just think 'why bother?'
> **Graham**: this isn't a one off, it's millions and millions of times ... if you meet somebody new, and you've got to tell them all this again ... when you've said it five million times in the past, you get a little bit irate, about half way through the story.

In fact, the explanations parents provide can just as easily back-fire:

> **Emma**: I don't like people sort of saying 'oh well .. he can't hear me because he's deaf', that really does annoy me. ... You get some .. and they'll say to me 'can he hear me?' that annoys me [too]. Well it shouldn't .. it doesn't annoy me, I don't know what it is really. It's not because I don't want to think he's deaf. Sometimes I think that's what people think. Like that I try to cover it up by, you know, just talking to him normal. Because he is normal, .. I want

other people to treat him as normal and that's what I try to get over to people. If he's being naughty [they might say] 'oh, you shouldn't do that because he's deaf' [but] deaf or not he's been naughty, he needs a smack.

We can see the disablement created as Emma struggles against prejudice about herself, as she tries to dismantle those constructed around her child.

Misleading comparisons

Yet other disabling images families met with consist in the myth that hearing impairment is somehow less problematic than other types of impairment:

> **Andrew**: people used to say 'oh, at least she's not blind'. .. A classic one, 'at least she's not blind'.
> **Helen**: 'At least she has brains.' 'At least she can walk.'

The image of deafness being less problematic than other impairments, is founded on ignorance of the extent to which disablement is created socially. No doubt, such interactions also arise from the difficulty people have in dealing with someone else's problem and trying to give some sort of reassurance from a basis of little experience or knowledge. Such reactions also smack of 'mustn't complain', however, and have the effect of belittling the barriers which deaf children and their families must face. Ironically such remarks, intended to reduce anxiety and distress, create disablement (Van der Klift and Kunc, 1994). Deaf children and their families may be crushed by such dismissals into supposing that they shouldn't expect other people to enable them:

> **Jenny**: she's not in pain or anything, like a lot of children are .. so we must get on with it.

Because hearing impairment is not always immediately obvious, deaf children and their families frequently find themselves marginalised:

> **Andrew**: [there is] this problem about deafness because if you've got a child who's Down's it's very visible or a blind child where everybody says 'oh, gosh', where society reacts more clearly. With deaf kids, of course, this is the .. paradox.

> **Maureen**: it doesn't register with people. If someone only had one eye or something, somebody can see that you couldn't see very well, but when you're deaf it doesn't register.

Assumptions about who disabled people are, may have to be grappled with:

135

Gillian: [you are invisible] if you speak normally. You draw attention to the fact if you sign .. you have got .. it's like a blind person's white stick or blank expression for want of a better description, it is something visible and obvious that you have got that says 'I'm slightly different from you. Please take notice or be aware of, that I'm different from you.'

Parents felt confused about how to contend with disabling imagery in order to enable their deaf child to develop an appropriate self-identity:

Jenny: people don't see deafness. You look at Chloe and she looks perfectly normal. A blind person has a white stick, you know then, don't you? Now I'm not saying I want to advertise that Chloe's deaf ... its hard to explain why I feel frustrated.

All of the families were aware of the need to resist stereotypical images of deafness which contribute to the disablement of their children. Christopher's parents spell this out:

Tony: if you have noticed we never say 'handicapped'. It's something we made our mind up about. Whether we're right or wrong, we never say 'handicapped' ... so I think really if you do have any problems shall we say ... then you've probably got to try that bit more to get a job or to get on in life, to be self-sufficient.

Pat: I'd like to see [Christopher] happily married with lots of children, whether hearing or deaf, as long as they are healthy. But with lots of certificates of achievements on the walls just to show those awful people who consider them as handicapped.

The word 'handicapped' connotes dependence and has nothing to do with the future Pat and Tony envisage for their child. As Tony says, to escape from the kind of unfulfilled future Barnes has labelled 'cabbage syndrome', Christopher will have to 'shall we say ... try that bit more' (Barnes, 1990). It would be preferable if other people could consider just what bit more they could do to enable children like Christopher.

Images of culture

Another set of assumptions which disable deaf children and their families concern images of culture. For deaf children born to hearing parents this issue is central. Deaf children may share language and experiences with d/Deaf people which their hearing family may not share. Arguments abound about the pros and cons of deaf children being equipped for a sense of belonging to both hearing and Deaf cultures. As with debates about communication, however, the arguments are often put emotively and parents are torn in many different directions. Tony recalls some

advice which captures this:

> **Tony**: [the teacher] advised us 'you've got two choices, you can either be a
> Deaf person in a Deaf world or you can be a deaf person in a hearing world'.

This picture is a glaring oversimplification and such a blunt division can
bring great pressure to bear on parents who could feel that they must
make a decision for their child so that they can be put on their 'chosen
path' from an early stage.

Gillian experienced the debate about inclusion of deaf children in the
cultures of Deaf versus hearing people as aggressive. This had led her to
some resentment of the Deaf Community whom she felt wrongly reject-
ed oral deaf children. Nevertheless, she respects her child's own choices
in the matter:

> **Gillian**: I mean she's my child and she belongs to my culture ... that famous
> word comes back ... and the Deaf culture is a different culture. They have ...
> not only have they got signing in common but a lot of them went away to col-
> lege, to school, at a very early age, they were brought up in a totally different
> environment. It's not just the communication thing, they've a lot of other
> things in common, that makes them a culture, a community, call it what you
> will ... she doesn't even necessarily have anything in common with [another
> deaf girl] ... now whether at a later date when they are adult or teenage they
> will find that communication point in common or will find the fact that
> they've got deafness in common an advantage or something that draws them
> together, I don't know.

Gillian is also aware of the political weight behind the strong moves from
the Deaf Community for recognition and equal opportunities (Corker,
1993; Ladd, 1991; Padden and Humphries, 1988) and is anxious that they
may not represent all deaf children:

> **Gillian**: I mean the Deaf, deaf with capital 'D', have got a lot of political
> clout, awareness. People are aware of Deafness and Deaf people, they have
> got a lot of clout, both from the information point of view, both from the sym-
> pathy *and* the political correctness point of view ... and I'm not totally critical
> of them, they have got a point of view ... [but] the way that they dismiss chil-
> dren like my Siân , and there must be an awful lot more of them too in the
> country, is very unfair.

This is a thorny area of discussion, as Gillian appreciates. She wants
equality for all deaf children, whether they are defined as part of the Deaf
or hearing world and does not want division or new stereotypes with
which to contend. At a time when sign language users, who have suffered
from years of oppression and discrimination, are gaining recognition and
respect for their rights, families with oral deaf children may fear the tide

threatens to sweep aside their interests.

Emma makes a pertinent point:

Emma: I'd like [Sam] to be able to understand the problem he's got and learn everything about it, just like I've learnt ... you know, see what he says about it, see how he feels about wearing hearing aids ... People don't take into account what parents think either, but the children rarely get a say of their own.

Dilemmas facing deaf children

Assumptions other people make obviously do influence how deaf children see themselves and the view they take of their hearing impairment. Siân, for example, having been faced with many barriers to inclusion at nine years of age had said 'I don't like being deaf', and Jenny too, had faced similar comments from Chloe:

Jenny: she'll say 'I don't like being deaf. Stop me being deaf.'

Sometimes Chloe raised questions about her hearing impairment and identity. Her sister explained:

Joanna: sometimes Chloe asks why she is deaf and we aren't, so we can't really say anything except that she is special and God chose her.

However, Chloe also knew that she did not want to be hearing:

Jenny: I said to her 'if you had a wish, would you wish to hear do you think?' And she went 'No, no, I won't like it. Loud.'

Enabling, as opposed to disabling environments make a substantial difference to how deaf children feel about themselves. We referred in the previous chapter to the time in early adolescence, when Katy was very angry with her mother about her deafness. Her father recalls at the same period another change:

Andrew: suddenly you didn't want to wear your hearing aid or you would hide it, or you would forget to change the batteries, so I think you were trying to say 'No, I'm not deaf.'

Katy recollects that she was confused about her identity and whether she belonged in the hearing or Deaf world:

Katy: before I went to Deaf school [Mum and Dad] both tried to get me to go to [the local] Deaf club to learn sign language ... after school. I refused. I refused because I [was] 14, because I [had] got quite a lot of hearing friends.

Katy's identity as a member of the hearing community, the one her parents belonged to and the one to which she was accustomed, came under threat when her parents realised she was struggling in an oral environment, and her need for self-preservation was strong. However, Katy then changed from a local school to a segregated boarding school. This was a catalyst to a major shift in her views of herself as a Deaf person:

> **Katy**: when I went to [the] Deaf school, then I realised and changed a lot. When I went to Deaf school, because it [was] my world, my language. And I [became] happy. When I went [there], I learnt sign language. I find sign language easier. Communication much easier. I got more stronger and stronger when I was learning sign language... I learnt a lot of things, I felt like, a bit too late.

When disabling barriers to communication were removed, Katy developed a clearer sense of her own place in the world. She emerged from the period of conflict with a positive identity as a Deaf person. When we met her, Katy was proud of her identity and eager to counteract those images of 'unseen deafness':

> **Katy**: the thing is we say always deafness is invisible. If I go to a club on my own, then my deaf friend arrives, says 'hello' [signed] and I try to sign, then [people know we are] deaf ... we need to have big hearing aids!

There may be more substantial barriers to developing a cultural identity for deaf children and their families who do not seek a sense of belonging within the Deaf Community:

> **Gillian**: I thought I would go out and talk to d/Deaf adults. 'Deaf' deaf, about Deaf Awareness. We would talk about this, and we'll find someone else who is deaf, who wears hearing aids, who is oral .. and you can't find them. And as a consequence, these kids aren't getting a positive role model, they are getting a negative role model because what they are doing isn't politically, morally, whatever, I don't know what the word is, correct ... and it doesn't do their self-confidence any good, it does not give them any positive feedback about themselves.

In addition, hearing parents with deaf children may find their own identity threatened by changing philosophies concerning their deaf child's cultural membership. However, as others have noted, the experience of d/Deaf people can inform and support parents in relation to these issues (Corker, 1994). Helen and Derek commented on their attitude swing over time:

> **Andrew**: we haven't had a lot to do with the Deaf Community but we're having more now.

Dilemmas facing parents

Parents with deaf children have to contend with a variety of threats to their own identity that come with being perceived as in need of professional help. Threats arise because the world of professional support which families with deaf children are placed in, involves many new situations, new information and unfamiliar people. Helen describes the changes which come about:

Helen: you become a handicapped family, there is no doubt about that.

Parents are expected to operate in ways and contexts which they may not previously have encountered. Gillian is aware that in this world of things unknown to the family, she might be labelled 'stupid'. But over the years she has decided her best chance of enabling Siân comes with ignoring what other people think:

Gillian: listening and thinking and asking questions and saying 'what's that for? I've never seen that before' .. and not being afraid to look stupid and ask questions about things because I mean you don't know, you can't, nobody knows everything, all there is to know about it, but you as a parent have got to be aware of these things.

Even when parents do have full information, they cannot guarantee they will be credited with this. Relief that Gillian describes when her GP accepts her expertise is a tell-tale sign of the oppressive barriers she has come to expect in such circumstances, when her role as parent in the parent–professional relationship is so often judged as the non-expert one with little valuable information to offer:

Gillian: he said to me 'you know more about it than me'. Of course that was a relief. You get an awful lot of doctors who simply dismiss you as not knowing what you're talking about ... you find that you are always battling up against somebody .. somebody's attitude or somebody's view.

When parents have to challenge images of themselves as dependent and naive, they are presented with yet another set of disabling barriers:

Pat: I want him to have the same opportunity but it's not easy because of other people ... you find that you've got to battle and fight for it and it gets a bit much sometimes but you've got to keep doing it.

Maureen: I'm always feeling that I've got to battle for him.

Families with deaf children clearly are prepared to fight long and hard against disabling images, stereotypes and prejudice. They would be greatly assisted if those in positions of power would examine assumptions they make, and values they hold. The effects of a single conflict with other people's preconceived ideas cannot be underestimated but the toll of numerous encounters with differing false images to counteract, is untold.

Professionals and others who support deaf children and their families can play an important part in enabling parents to discuss some of the experiences they are facing, and by keeping the negative and disabling effect of stereotypes in mind. Most of the families we met were able to tell us of individual professionals who had helped them and given their self-image a much needed boost. For example, the teacher supporting Siân's family conveyed that she trusted and respected the family's capabilities for making up their own mind about oralism:

> **Gillian**: she said 'try it, see what they've got for her'. She knows us, she knows we stay calm and we are not such people to take anybody's extremities of belief on board without questioning it.

Emma had also found some service providers a source of empowerment:

> **Emma**: yes, you know what to do, you know sort of who to ask for and who to speak to and it's only through [going to the new service] they've given me ideas and the courage to do them myself.

With commitment, professionals can and do resist disabling images of deaf children and their families and this clearly makes a world of difference.

Having explored some of the barriers which disabling imagery presents to deaf children and their families, we shall now turn to a consideration of just how these barriers impact on their hopes and dreams of the future.

Enabling futures

Parents interspersed their recollections with their aspirations for their deaf child in future relationships, in employment and in community life. Jenny's experiences of disablement were so wide-ranging that she felt Chloe might need a hearing partner to overcome obstacles in later life:

> **Jenny**: I don't want her to marry someone who is deaf. I know I'm being selfish here, but this is my idea for her, for the simple reason that a hearing person would be more capable of looking after her. Because there is lots of sort of things .. obstacles that occur to you for a deaf person, but two deaf people ... The chances are she will marry someone deaf, I know. I'm not going to object and say 'you're not marrying that deaf person' but I am aware that I'd like her to marry a hearing person.

Jenny knows that there are 'obstacles ... for a deaf person'. These consist in the negative images, barriers to communication and hurdles in the way of inclusion which the family have come up against throughout Chloe's life. Understandably, Jenny fears disablement will be compounded for two deaf people together. Secondly, in common with other parents who have children who are disabled, she also recognises, in the face of so many barriers, a great desire in herself to be reassured about who will carry on the role of looking after her daughter, because she has little reason to believe barriers are being dismantled (McCormack, 1992). At odds with Jenny's awareness of Chloe's dependence, however, is her desire to enable independence:

> **Jenny**: I'd like her to have a good job ... and .. just be happy. I want her happy, and I want to know that she can survive without us.

There is nothing connected with hearing impairment that means d/Deaf people cannot work, and be happy, but there is prejudice and discrimination to overcome en route. Gillian reflected on barriers to employment for young d/Deaf people:

> **Gillian**: you occasionally come across a job description or somebody will say 'oh, that's an interesting job' and I'll think 'oh, Siân couldn't do that'. ... It does cross your mind now and again, 'Siân might find that difficult.' Simple little things, you know, that communication might cause a barrier to. But then on the other hand, she has got her self-confidence not to be phased by it, or if she decides that that's what she ought to do she will go ahead and twist, bugger what anybody else thinks about it you know ... fair play to her, and if that's what she wants to do, I would never stop her from doing anything or dissuade her from doing something.

We have talked elsewhere about the resourcefulness of deaf children and their families in achieving high goals in respect of education, training and employment in the post-school years (Moore and Beazley, 1992). However, school leavers with impairments face prejudice and discrimination in the labour market and many environmental and attitudinal barriers threaten their attainments. Tony and Pat were aware from their understanding of deafness and the disadvantages that deaf people encounter, that Christopher will be confronted with difficulties:

> **Tony**: I just want to know he's quite capable of being a citizen to the full if you like, ... and enjoying, happy
> **Pat**: there are certain things he can't do because ..
> **Tony**: because he can't hear .. I mean it's difficult now to get a job. So I think really if you do have any problems shall we say ... then you've probably got to try that bit more to get a job or to get on in life, to be self-sufficient.

But the things Christopher 'can't do because .. he can't hear' are things Christopher could do if work places were adapted to the needs of people with hearing impairment. Once again, the barriers do not lie within the child, but within other people's attitudes and obstacles which society places in Christopher's way. Gillian makes this argument:

> **Gillian**: I don't worry about *her*. What I worry about is *other people's attitudes* to her that's all. Will she in the future find people who are sympathetic enough [or] there's nothing you can change? Things you can change aren't so bad. You can change if it needs changing if you are aware of it, you can change. [I'm dreading her] being an adult, whether that's going to alienate her or knock her confidence sort of or undo all the good work that we've done so far, I don't know. I mean you can't predict the future. ... You could worry yourself about all sorts and get paranoid couldn't you? We will deal with it. And being aware of what might happen I suppose is good.

Gillian expresses real anxiety over Siân's future because she fears other people will deny her access. She feels Siân will be dependent on the good-will of others and this is fundamentally unsatisfactory. Deaf children and their families need to be assured that a fulfilling future is as much their right as anybody else's and professionals have a key role to play in bringing about necessary change.

The children who we spoke to all had their own ideas of the future and their chosen careers:

> **Siân**: be a nurse ... I want to join the other nurses.

> **Rachel**: a teacher .. I'm not sure, perhaps a swimming teacher.

> **Chloe**: a hairdresser.

> **Katy**: in the Theatre of the Deaf .. I could be an interpreter .. I might, I might. I like [interpreting opera]. Some people think I couldn't do it because I'm deaf, have to be hearing .. that's a big problem.

As Katy knows, the biggest obstacle is not hearing impairment, but assumptions other people make about d/Deaf people. Enabling environments are the key to Katy's dreams coming true:

> **Helen**: I see her doing well and I just see her being OK but she will always need help from somebody
> **Derek**: support
> **Katy**: when filling in .. like application forms for a job or an actor. I ask for help [with] difficult words. Used to [ask] my parents, now my boyfriend will have to help me.

In our previous study of prospects for young d/Deaf people after leaving school, we found that deaf children can indeed enter into the full range of professions to which hearing people have access, and to which those in our study aspire (Moore and Beazley, 1992). However, they have to overcome a huge range of barriers along the way and preparation for leaving school often leaves much to be desired. Of course, barriers to work will be a product of barriers experienced in education and the role of schools in preparation for work is inestimable. Ian, for example, wants to be a chef, and the following passage reveals his family are supportive of, and enthusiastic about, his aim:

> **Graham**: he's into cooking [laughs] he loves cooking .. you should see him in the kitchen! My goodness! He's doing his mock O levels next year, they're doing the run up to them now .. and one of Ian's courses is cookery and he has to plan a whole hour ... everything from what you've got to get, to what washing up's got to be done in this hour. He's only done one last week, don't know how he got on ... I can just imagine
> **Maureen**: [laughs] at least he does that at school!
> **Graham**: yeah ... he makes a mess, Maureen has to keep on to him, 'wash it, wash it'
> **Maureen**: he don't get the hours quite right!
> **Graham**: you can say that again [laughter].

Ian faces barriers to a fulfilling career of his choice, however, if access to further education is denied. Families expressed concern about the extent to which their children's ambitions will be enabled, or not, by factors beyond their control:

> **Tony**: if you talk to the average lad he wants to be either a sailor or an airman or a fireman, or a police man .. they all go through that stage, and I think it's all ready dawned on [Christopher] that he can't do things like that. He won't be able to do things like that so he's got that kind of in mind.

Low expectations of deaf school leavers can particularly block their ambitions. One parent wrote about this, describing how her son's experience of prejudice imposed barriers to earning a living and severely knocked his self-esteem:

> **Anon**: [our son] really wanted to be a builder. He was heart broken when firm after firm turned him down because he was deaf. We sat through several *very* depressing meetings. I suspect the people involved forgot that the interpreter was passing on to [him] all their dismal comments re: the state of the economy, unemployment etc.

This provides a powerful illustration of how stereotypical images of deaf people produce disablement. 'The people involved' disable young d/Deaf people by failing to consider how they might create a barrier-free working environment. Undoubtedly, disabling images play a critical role in determining deaf children's access to equal opportunities, to full citizenship and to a fulfilling future of their own choice.

Summary

In this chapter we have tried to examine the impact of prejudice and disabling imagery on the lives of deaf children and their families. Assumptions and stereotypes are seen to be profoundly oppressive because they pitch deaf children and their families in a continual battle against disablement.

The challenge which we feel is raised, is for others to start addressing this complex area of oppression through examining personal beliefs and values and developing open discussion. When deaf children and their families find their sense of personal identity under threat and their futures blocked it is helpful if they can know it is not hearing impairment which stands in the way of significant living and a fulfilling future. Disabling barriers are socially created and need to be dismantled. A major part of the dismantling process consists in knowing what to expect and why and then strategies can be evolved for enablement, not disablement. The key to a fulfilling life for deaf children and their families lies in minimising prejudice and fear of hearing impairment both within and beyond the family.

DISMANTLING BARRIERS

Families

Take a look at popular representations of children in newspapers and magazines for example, or on the television, advertisement hoardings and the charity appeal envelopes that come through your door. What messages come across about the children? What images of deaf children are presented? Can you think of more enabling ways in which images of deaf children could be put across?

Consider how your family, perhaps with other local people, could devise an awareness activity in your area to present positive images of deaf children and their families. You could for instance focus on a school or play-group, or encourage children to set up a poster campaign in a GP surgery. Talk to other people about why popular images of deaf children matter and ask them to help you.

Professionals

As suggested above, take a look at popular representations of children. What images of deaf children are presented? Can you think of more enabling ways in which images of deaf children could be put across? What steps can you take to create more enabling images of deaf children in your own work?

Consider how you and like-minded colleagues could set about raising awareness and presenting positive images of deaf children and their families. Talk to other people about why popular images of deaf children matter and ask them to help you.

CHAPTER 7
What Can Be Done?

Introduction

Our main purpose in this book has been to show how the reactions and attitudes of other people can have a profound impact upon the lives of deaf children and their families. What we have found is that it is not the fact that a child has a hearing impairment which threatens to plunge them and their family into personal tragedy. Rather it is the way in which other people react, together with the availability of supportive services, that determines the extent to which they will be immersed in suffering or conversely, be able to lead an ordinary life. We have said before that our concern is not to dispute that hearing impairment can have a profound impact upon children and their families, but rather to show that it is the nature of support which determines whether a child's hearing impairment is associated with tragedy or not. We feel the material presented in this book does show how easy it is to make the experience of deafness disabling, not just for hearing-impaired children, but for their families too. It also shows that this is not inevitable and that hearing parents regard their deaf children as a precious gift, just as Oliver has reported Ladd as saying that the Deaf Community do (Oliver, 1993b).

Before going on to look at some of the implications of our study, it is necessary to mention some of its limitations.

Limitations of the study

Firstly, our study was based on a small group of self-referring families. Despite this, we believe that the material presented highlights sufficiently wide-ranging issues for it to be applicable to a great many deaf children and their families, and those living with other impairments too. We fear, however, that most policy makers remain firmly attached to the fantasy of collecting 'objective' data; they prefer statistical conclusions and may be reluctant to accept ways in which the research reported here has benefited, we think enormously, by distance from the conventional approach to data collection.

We are happy to admit that the information we obtained simply gives rise to one particular way of seeing things. Service providers may dispute whether we have presented 'the real picture', but we will argue that this does not actually matter. The most important aim has been to prompt readers to challenge their own way of looking at things. We could have administered a 'scientifically valid' and 'reliable' questionnaire, perhaps sent to hundreds of families, and then presented the kind of hard numbers which policy makers traditionally set store by. But we feel sure that a report on percentages of families who would, for example, 'like more information at the point of diagnosis', or 'need more advice when deciding about communication', would provide far less insight into the needs of deaf children and their families than the in-depth reflections we have presented instead. And whether or not the accounts presented here are regarded as 'valid' and 'reliable,' simply depends, of course, on what your own subjective view of 'science' is anyway (Hammersly, 1993; Holloway, 1989; Woolgar, 1988).

We have presented a true picture of what the families we met told us with minimal stripping down of their accounts. We would not deny that we have our own motivations for presenting issues in a particular way, but we hope we have sufficiently prioritised what families themselves have had to say, for this book to consist, as far as possible, of the messages they wanted to get across. Certainly there is not much of what they said left on the cutting room floor.

The second reservation we wish to point out is that a better project would undoubtedly be built from a stronger involvement of deaf children and their families in its design and inception. The original idea came from the young d/Deaf people we interviewed in previous research and also Deaf consultants involved with that project (Moore and Beazley, 1992). However, financial constraints made it impossible to facilitate the full involvement of deaf children and their families in the stages of design and analysis. Several writers who challenge researchers to involve disabled people more equitably in their enquiries do themselves recognise the lack of autonomy often available for this purpose in practice, but nevertheless, this omission does create limitations (Oliver, 1993c; Parker and Baldwin, 1992).

Despite these reservations, however, we believe our study provides important scope for some suggestions as to how deaf children and their families can be enabled to get what they want and need out of services provided in the future.

Bringing about change

In an ideal world, when families refer to problems that everyone who

works with deaf children and their families feels they have heard count-
less times, parents would not remain tormented by the question 'why
should other people go through it?' (Graham). There is, however, a long
way to go before disabling physical environments and oppressive attitudes will be fully dismantled. In the meantime, what can hard-pressed
but well-intentioned individuals do to bring about desired changes?

The major barrier which needs to be dismantled is the oppressive
mythology which allows service providers to think in terms of the personal inadequacies of deaf children and their families. Families have
revealed how such an individual approach to deaf children and their families generates a smoke screen through which professionals can filter out
blame for their own short-comings and defend their own practice even if
is not proving enabling. Deaf children and their families do not share
exactly the same needs, but they do share the same entitlement to getting
those needs met. When Graham asks 'do you think everything you're
doing will make any change, make anything better?' we feel that the
development of more enabling support lies in the willingness of service
providers to take a social view of disability and stop assuming that the
problems lie with deaf children and families.

A parent who has articulated many thoughts on how professionals can
promote enablement in this book, describes how much professionals can
learn from listening to parents about the source of difficulties they, and
their children, encounter:

> **Gillian**: I went to [a] conference annual general meeting, and they had a very
> good afternoon with the pick of the professionals more or less, heads and pro-
> fessionals that was the type ... they had really good speakers who obviously
> on the professional side were very good ... they were aware of all the current
> things. And they had two ladies at the end of the afternoon who sat on the
> front desk, they didn't rehearse, they had no overhead projector or slides ...
> they just sat and told people, like I told you, *what actually happened to me
> and how I felt about it*. And there was a conference hall with .. it must have
> been a 150 people and all the parents are going 'yes!' And the vast majority
> of the professionals had tears in their eyes because they just did not realise
> how emotionally it affected people. And it was very brave of them. [One of
> the parent-speakers] was upset. She churned it out the way I churned it out to
> you and it might seem as though I'm harping on about it, but every single pro-
> fessional that night talked to everybody about the same thing. And I churn out
> that story because ... the people who are on the other side of the table don't
> necessarily hear it.

Clearly professionals shouldn't resign themselves to being on the receiving end of criticism from families. Gillian's story is fascinating because it
reveals how when professionals actually do empower families, and listen

to what they say, instead of relinquishing power, they can actually reclaim it.

When professionals do not empower deaf children and their families, however, through failing to take parents seriously, or exploiting the trappings of professionalism, they may feel more powerful, and they may get to dictate what form support of families takes, but in doing so, professionals actually lose power, forfeit respect and, of course, oppress families:

> **Gillian**: oh, I've dismissed the professionals as complete and utter waste of time [laughs]. I treat them with the contempt they deserve. I would question them at all points of the compass. ... I'm not that militant about it but I have a healthy scepticism, that's the word, for anything that medical or other professionals do. I am aware of their biases and points of view and all that. I like to think that I'm fairly balanced in my attitudes about them, but I can if you like, play devil's advocate when necessary with officials [laughs] ... I don't think it does anybody any harm to wind them up but it probably gives me a label of being a bit of a stirrer so I can't win. You can't win, no matter whose side of the fence you sit on.

Through disempowering families, professionals automatically disempower themselves, with frustrating results all round. Most of all, however, there is damage which rebounds on deaf children:

> **Gillian**: to me, this is where the professionals could come in, if they were more aware of what might happen. It's where their responsibility lies and they should be on top of these things ... I feel that's where they've let me down in a way and that they really shouldn't have done that. And they should have been ... it's working together as a team effort ... it's hopeless. We are in the middle somewhere, you know. You have to shout at them to get them to do anything, you know, it's quite pathetic. But then if you don't work as a team, it's the kids in the middle who will miss out.

We have seen elsewhere in this book that parents can be so disempowered that they are unable to seek out support to which they are entitled:

> **Maureen**: I think a lot of people don't fight, they just accept it
> **Graham**: they're not encouraged to fight because they haven't got the information.

We have speculated that perhaps it actually suits professionals to oppress families. Ironically, as we have seen, however, keeping parents in the dark, or seeking to manipulate them in other ways does not suppress their needs. It simply creates more. There are many lessons for all service providers here:

> **Gillian**: I appreciate that ... we just can't afford [everything deaf children and

their families want] basically, but then on the other hand it doesn't mean you've got to be complacent and think your service is the best thing since sliced bread.

We are conscious that the things families have said could be seen as anti-professional. Parents themselves were aware of this, apologising, for example, if '[this] might sound like professional bashing' or 'like the band wagon'. But as Oliver points out 'because services are designed without their input, they often turn out to be inappropriate. Then, when disabled people dare to criticise, they are accused of being .. anti-professional' (Oliver, 1993a).

It might be worth mentioning that Andrew and Helen, and Eleanor all had a dual perspective as parents of deaf children who were also professionals in family support and education services. These parents were often commenting on what was wrong with the system as *insider* representatives of those systems. They valued the work they did, but also recognised the dilemmas inherent in their positions. As parents in receipt of those same services, they could see why families might be dissatisfied with provision. We include ourselves in this group, in our roles as both researchers and professionals.

Family friendly policy

Emphasis in the Children Act (1989), on the development of services which are responsive to the views of children and their parents may help to address some of the issues identified, but in order for this to happen, the concerns of deaf children and their families must first be elicited in meaningful ways. In addition, the 1993 Code of Practice on 'special educational needs' (sic) increasingly requires service providers to promote partnerships with parents and children (Davie, 1993). The task for those working for deaf children and their families, is to develop practice which attends to the experience of impairment without manufacturing oppression, and recent legislation does provide some enhanced emphasis on enabling this.

The hindered passage of anti-discrimination legislation, however, is widely regarded as a major variable currently determining the continued disablement and oppression of deaf children and their families (Oliver and Barnes, 1993). Such legislation would enable many of the barriers deaf children and their families face to be challenged. Ian's experience, for example, of being called 'deafo' is uniquely without recourse to protection. Current legislation protects children from abuse on the grounds of race or gender but not from abuse relating to impairment. Without name-calling, Ian and his family might be more comfortable with mainstream schooling. With barrier-free inclusive education, Ian could have access to the career of his choice. With a career of his choice, he would have the means to carve out an independently chosen and fulfilling future which would disprove negative images of deaf children and their achievements, and so on. Anti-discrimination legislation, is essential if institutional oppression of deaf children and their families is to be dismantled. The perpetual delays to the passage of such legislation, however, lend support to the recurring theme in this book whereby we argue that people who do not live with impairments may have vested interests in reproducing vulnerability for those who do. Of course, even full civil rights legislation will not alleviate the barriers deaf children and their families face. An even greater challenge lies in creating a society which deplores discrimination and oppression (Barnes and Oliver, 1995).

What else do we need to find out?

Like the families we met, representatives from the National Deaf Children's Society and others, we feel that a lot would be gained from gathering the views of deaf children themselves. Some researchers have asked children about certain aspects of their lives, such as identity (Smith, 1993), or explored a range of pre-determined issues such as communication skills, identity and self-esteem (Gregory, 1994), but on the whole 'little is known specifically about [deaf] children's views ... on how they perceive the approach used by professionals responsible for their development' (Bench, 1992).

In this book, we have been able to include some ideas from children themselves but there is much more deaf children can offer in the way of opinions, feelings and suggestions. Careful consideration needs to be given to the ways in which young people and very young children can be enabled to put their own views forward (Fivush and Hudson, 1990; Westcott, 1992). A great deal of professional practice concentrates upon children's needs but as we have seen, these supposed needs are presented in particular ways (Lynas, 1994). Doubtless, deaf children's own stories would shed light on what *they* really want from their lives and what *in their view* would enable them to attain their dreams and goals.

It would also be valuable to seek the views of families who face a wide range of social barriers such as those of race and culture in addition to those created around their child's impairment. Families from cultural and linguistic minority groups, which might also include those where the parents are d/Deaf, are generally under-represented in social research. It is well known that patterns of service provision often operate to the disadvantage of people from cultural and linguistic minority groups and that professionals often lack awareness of different cultural values (MIND, 1992). The need for studies which examine culturally diverse families with sensitivity and relevance is pressing (Dilworth-Anderson *et al.*, 1993).

A final area which we strongly believe deserves further attention, is the monitoring of changes in personal power that occur when deaf children and their families are listened to, and the outcomes of dismantling some of the barriers that might have been constructed by others around them. If an equally chance selection of deaf children and their families came forward to participate in a repeat of this study in ten years time, will we again find ourselves reporting difficulties which service providers have heard tell of time and time again, yet have continued to do nothing about?

What can you do to make a difference?

We hope that parents, professionals and others reading this book will be prompted to think through their own experiences and to consider ways in which services could become more enabling in their support. Deaf people, including children, and their families and professionals working with them, who may have felt angry or disappointed in parts of this book, will hopefully recognise that there is a tremendous amount that can be done to prevent the repetition of certain parts of the stories from families reported here and to ensure the construction of enabling experiences.

The main thing we have realised as a result of listening to the families, is that their aspirations are for an ordinary life, and they are not thwarted in this by hearing impairment, but by oppressive attitudes and disabling environments which must be challenged without delay.

DISMANTLING BARRIERS

Families and professionals

Consider the following extract:

Sunday 10th November [from Jenny's diary]
Well I thought we'd have had a frightened little girl on Tuesday, bonfire night, but not at all. Dad lit the bonfire in the back garden while the children and I watched through the window. I turned round to pick Chloe up and she'd disappeared, so I followed the noises coming from the hall and there stood Chloe tugging frantically at her duffel coat. She'd already donned her wellies, on the wrong feet might I add, and by goodness that little girl wasn't being restricted to the indoors, so after words of warning, all three got togged up for the outdoors. Then, with an outstretched arm, Chloe made herself quite plain that she wanted to hold a sparkler, which she did, and loved every minute. In fact, when Shelly came running into the kitchen in floods of tears, Chloe gave a look of puzzlement as to say 'what's all the fuss?' Bonfire Night gave us another first of the year as well, yes it actually snowed. Chloe does not like this and shows no sign whatsoever of changing her mind.

References

Baetens-Beardsmore, H. (1993) *European Models of Bilingual Education*. Clevedon: Multilingual Matters.

Baker, C. (1993) *Foundations of Bilingual Education and Bilingualism*. Clevedon: Multilingual Matters.

Barnes, C. (1990) *Cabbage Syndrome: the Social Construction of Dependence*. Basingstoke, Hants: Falmer Press.

Barnes, C. (1992) *Disabling Imagery and the Media: an Exploration of the Principles for Media Representations of Disabled People*. British Council of Disabled People. Halifax: Ryburn Publishing.

Barnes, C. and Oliver, M. (1995), 'Disability rights: rhetoric and reality in the UK', *Disability and Society*, 10 (1), pp. 111–16.

Barton, L. (1993) 'Labels, markets and inclusive education', in Visser, J. and Upton, G. (eds) *Special Education in Britain After Warnock*. London: David Fulton Publishers.

Barton, L. (1994) 'Segregated education: some critical observations'. Paper presented at *Removing Disabling Barriers Conference*, London: Policy Studies Institute.

Bench, R. J. (1992) *Communication Skills in Hearing-Impaired Children*. London: Whurr.

Bouvet, D. (1990) *The Path to Language: Bilingual Education for Deaf Children*. Clevedon: Multilingual Matters.

British Deaf Association (1995) 'BDA Policy on Cochlear Implants', *Laserbeam*, 23, Winter 1994/5, pp. 34–5.

Burman, E. (1994) *Deconstructing Developmental Psychology*. London: Routledge.

Clark, M. (1989) *Language through Living for Hearing Impaired Children*. London: Hodder & Stoughton.

Corker, M. (1993) 'Integration and deaf people', in Swain, J., Finkelstein, V., French, S. and Oliver, M. (eds) *Disabling Barriers – Enabling Environments*. London: Sage.

Corker, M. (1994) *Counselling: the Deaf Challenge*. London: Jessica Kingsley.

Cummins, J. and Swain, M. (1986) *Bilingualism in Education*. London: Longman.

154

Davie, R. (1993) 'Editorial: the Education Act 1993', *British Journal of Special Education*, 20 (3).

Davis, K. (1993) 'The crafting of good clients', in Swain, J., Finkelstein, V., French, S. and Oliver, M. (eds), *Disabling Barriers – Enabling Environments*. London: Sage.

Department of Health (1991) *The Children Act: Guidance and Regulations*, Vols 2 and 6. London: HMSO.

Dilworth-Anderson, P., Burton, M. and Turner, W. (1993) 'The importance of values in the study of culturally diverse families', *Family Relations*, 42 (3).

Dyson, S. (1987) 'Reasons for assessment: rhetoric and reality in the assessment of children with disabilities', in Booth, T. and Swann, W. (eds) *Including Pupils with Disabilities*. Milton Keynes: Open University Press.

Finkelstein, V. (1993) *Being Disabled*, Workbook 1; K665, The Disabling Society. Milton Keynes: The Open University.

Fivush, R. and Hudson, J.A. (1990) *Knowing and Remembering in Young Children*. New York: Cambridge University Press.

Fletcher, L. (1987) *Language for Ben: a Deaf Child's Right to Sign*. London: Souvenir Press.

Foster, S. (1989) 'Reflections of a group of deaf adults on their experiences in mainstream and residential school programmes in the United States', *Disability, Handicap and Society*, 4 (1), pp. 37–56.

Freeman, A. (1988) 'Parents: dilemmas for professionals', *Disability, Handicap and Society*, 3 (1), pp. 79–85.

French, S. (1993) *Dismantling the Barriers*, Workbook 3; K665, *The Disabling Society*. Milton Keynes: The Open University.

Gallaway, C. and Woll, B. (1994) 'Interaction and childhood deafness', in Gallaway, C. and Richards, B. (eds) *Input and Interaction in Language Acquisition*. Cambridge: Cambridge University Press.

Gregory, S. (1976) *The Deaf Child and his Family*. London: Allen and Unwin.

Gregory, S. (1991) 'Challenging motherhood: mothers and their deaf children', in Phoenix, A., Woollett, A. and Lloyd, E. (eds) *Motherhood: Meanings, Practice and Ideologies*. London: Sage.

Gregory, S. (1994) 'The developing deaf child', in Laurenzi, C. and Hindley, P. (eds) *Keep Deaf Children in Mind*. Leeds: The National Deaf Children's Society Family Centre.

Hammersly, M. (ed.) (1993) *Research Methods: Philosophy, Politics and Practice*. London: Sage/Open University.

Holloway, W. (1989) *Subjectivity and Method in Psychology*. London: Sage.

155

Hornby, G. (1992) 'A review of fathers' accounts of their experiences parenting children with disabilities', *Disability, Handicap and Society*, 7 (4), pp. 363–74.

Karmiloff-Smith, A. (1994) *Baby, It's You*. London: Ebury Press.

Keise, C. (1993) 'Developing a whole school approach for dealing with bullying in primary school', in Claire, H., Maybin, J. and Swann, J. (eds) *Equality Matters: Case Studies from the Primary School*. Clevedon: Multilingual Matters.

Keith, L. (1994) *Mustn't Grumble*. London: The Women's Press.

Kittel, R. (1991) 'Total commitment to total communication', in Taylor, G. and Bishop, J. (eds) *Being Deaf: the Experience of Deafness*. London: Pinter.

Kluwin, T. N. and Gaustad, M. G. (1991) 'Predicting family communication choices' *Am Ann Deaf*, 136, pp. 28–34.

Ladd, P. (1988) 'The modern deaf community', in Gregory, S. and Hartley, G. (eds) *Constructing Deafness*. London: Pinter.

Ladd, P. (1991) 'The erosion of social and self-identity', in Montgomery, G. (ed.) *The Integration and Disintegration of the Deaf in Society*. Scottish Workshop Publications.

Lane, H. (1991) 'Why the Deaf are angry', in Gregory, S. and Hartley, G. (eds) *Constructing Deafness*. London: Pinter.

Lane, H. (1994) 'The cochlear implant controversy', *Laserbeam*, 23, Winter 1994/5, pp. 27–33.

Laurenzi, C. (1994) 'The family', in Laurenzi, C. and Hindley, P. (eds) *Keep Deaf Children in Mind*. Leeds: The National Deaf Children's Society Family Centre.

Laurenzi, C. and Hindley, P. (eds) (1994) *Keep Deaf Children in Mind*. Leeds: The National Deaf Children's Society Family Centre.

Luterman, D. (1987) *Deafness in the Family*. Boston, MA: College Hill Press.

Lynas, W. (1994) *Communication Options in the Education of Deaf Children*. London: Whurr.

Lynas, W., Huntington, A. and Tucker, I. (1987) *A Critical Examination of Different Approaches to Communication in the Education of Deaf Children*. Rochdale: The Ewing Foundation.

McCormack, M. (1992) *Special Children, Special Needs: Families Talk about Living with Mental Handicap*. Wellingborough: Thorson.

McCormick, B. (1988) *Screening for Hearing Impairment in Young Children*. Beckenham: Croom Helm.

McCormick, B. (1993) 'Behavioural hearing tests 6 months to 3;6 years', in McCormick, B. (ed.) *Paediatric Audiology 0–5 Years*. London: Whurr.

McCracken, W. and Sutherland, H. (1991) *Deaf-ability Not Disability.* Clevedon: Multilingual Matters.

Meherali, R. (1994) 'Being black and deaf', in Laurenzi, C. and Hindley, P. (eds) *Keep Deaf Children in Mind.* Leeds: The National Deaf Children's Society Family Centre.

MIND (1992) *Black and Minority Ethnic Communities and Mental Health.* London: MIND Information.

Moore, M. (1993) *Opportunities for Communication in Integrated Settings: Young Deaf Children.* PhD Thesis: University of Greenwich.

Moore, M. and Beazley, S. (1992) *The Post-school Reflections of Young Deaf People.* Manchester Polytechnic Research Report.

Morris, J. (1991) *Pride Against Prejudice: Transforming Attitudes to Disability.* London: The Women's Press.

Morris, J. (1993) *Independent Lives.* London: Macmillan.

National Deaf Children's Society (1993) 'Schools out: hopes and dreams on leaving school', *TALK.*

Nolan, M. and Tucker, I. (1988) *The Hearing Impaired Child and the Family.* London: Souvenir Press.

Ogden, P. (1984) 'Parenting in the mainstream', *Volta Review*, 86, pp. 29–39.

Oliver, M. (1990) *The Politics of Disablement.* London: Macmillan.

Oliver, M. (1993a) 'Redefining disability: a challenge to research', in Swain, J., Finkelstein, V., French, S. and Oliver, M. (eds), *Disabling Barriers – Enabling Environments.* London: Sage.

Oliver, M. (1993b) 'Citizenship and welfare', *Disability, Citizenship and Empowerment*, Workbook 2, K665, The Disabling Society. Milton Keynes: The Open University.

Oliver, M. (1993c) 'Conductive education: if it wasn't so sad it would be funny', in Swain, J., Finkelstein, V., French, S. and Oliver, M. (eds) *Disabling Barriers – Enabling Environments.* London: Sage.

Oliver, M. and Barnes, C. (1993) 'Discrimination, disability and welfare: from needs to rights', in Swain, J., Finkelstein, V., French, S. and Oliver, M. (eds) *Disabling Barriers – Enabling Environments.* London: Sage.

Oliver, M., Zarb, G., Silver, J., Moore, M. and Salisbury, V. (1987) *Walking into Darkness.* London: Macmillan.

Padden, C. and Humphries, T. (1988) *Deaf in America: Voices from a Culture.* Cambridge, MA: Harvard University Press.

Parker, G. and Baldwin, S. (1992) 'Confessions of a jobbing researcher', *Disability, Handicap and Society*, 7 (2), pp. 197–203.

Pickersgill, M. (1990a) 'Bilingualism and the education of deaf children: Part 1. Theories, models and factors', *Deafness and Development*, 1

(1), pp. 10–14.

Pickersgill, M. (1990b) 'Bilingualism and the education of deaf children: Part 2. Implications and practical considerations', *Deafness and Development*, 1 (2), pp. 3–8.

Pickersgill, M. (1991) 'Bilingualism and the education of deaf children: Part 3. Towards a model of good practice', *Deafness and Development*, 2 (1), pp. 4–9.

Pound, L. and Moore, M. (1989) 'Integration: a pre-school case study', in Evans, R. (ed.) *Special Educational Needs: Policy and Practice*. Oxford: Blackwell.

Riseborough, G. (1993) 'Recent policy, the numbers game and the schooling of the hearing-impaired: a study of one teacher's career', *European Journal of Special Needs Education*, 8 (2), pp. 134–52.

Scanlon, P. and Bamford, J. (1990) 'Early identification of hearing loss: screening of surveillance methods', *Archives of Diseases in Childhood*, 65, pp. 479–85.

Schmidt-Rohlfing, B. (1993) 'Signing in class', in Claire, H., Maybin, J. and Swann, J. (eds) *Equality Matters: Case Studies from the Primary School*. Clevedon: Multilingual Matters.

Silo, J. (1994) 'The impact of school', in Laurenzi, C. and Hindley, P. (eds) *Keep Deaf Children in Mind*. Leeds: The National Deaf Children's Society Family Centre.

Smith, S. (1993) 'Self and identity of deaf children in bilingual education'. Paper presented at a seminar on *Developments in Bilingual Education*. Castle College, Sheffield, December.

Solity, J. and Bickler, G. (1994) *Support Services: Issues for Health and Social Services Professionals*. London: Cassell.

Van der Klift, E. and Kunc, N. (1994) 'Hell-bent on helping: benevolence, friendship and the politics of help', in Thousand, J., Villa, R. and Nevin, A. (eds) *Creativity and Collaborative Learning: a Practical Guide to Empowering Students and Teachers*. Baltimore: Paul Brooks.

Webster, A. (1986) *Deafness, Development and Literacy*. London: Methuen.

Webster, A. (1994) 'Hearing impairment', in Solity, J. and Bickler, G. (eds) *Support Services: Issues for Health and Social Services Professionals*. London : Cassell.

Webster, A. and Wood, D. (1989) *Children with Hearing Difficulties*. London: Cassell.

Wells, G. (1987) *The Meaning Makers: Children Learning Language and Using Language to Learn*. London: Hodder & Stoughton.

Westcott, H. (1992) 'The disabled child witness'. Poster presented at

158

NATO Advanced Studies Institute, *The Child Witness in Context: Cognitive, Social and Legal Perspectives*. Lucca, Italy.

Wickham-Searle, P. (1992) 'Careers in caring: mothers of children with disabilities', *Disability, Handicap and Society*, 7 (1), pp. 5–17.

Woolgar, S. (1988) *Science, the Very Idea*. London: Routledge.

Index